ADVERTISE LIKE A WARRIOR

POWERFUL ADVERTISING TACTICS FOR MODERN MEDIA BUYERS

10 PROVEN PERFORMANCE MARKETING STRATEGIES FOR ADS THAT CONVERT

Aman Verma

Made with ♥ on the Notion Press Platform

www.notionpress.com

Contents

Preface

These days, advertising is more than just catchy slogans and flashy pictures. It's about understanding complicated human behavior, using data to make choices, and tapping into emotional connections. This book is about learning how to balance these things perfectly. At its core, it is a useful guide for business owners, marketers, and anyone else who wants to learn how to make ads that sell in the digital age.

During a time of big change in the business world, the idea for this book began to take shape. As AI-powered tools and social media sites have become more popular over the last few years, I've seen a clear change in how people interact with brands. The old ways of marketing, which seemed to work every time, started to fail when people became smarter and pickier. It was clear that we needed new strategies—ones that combined imagination with data and took into account how complicated modern media is. This understanding made me want to write down the methods and plans that have worked in this new environment. I wanted to share these methods not only as lessons learned but also as a way for other people to follow.

It was very personal for me to write this book. There were many places where I wrote it, from busy coffee shops to the peace of my home office at midnight. Each one gave me a diverse inspiration. I stayed involved in the world I was writing about, whether I was watching how people behave while I was out and about or thinking about the details of a campaign while I was up late writing. This is the result: a collection of real-life tips, tricks, and ideas that will help both marketers and business owners.

I wrote this book because I know how hard it can be to find your way around the constantly changing world of ads. There has never been more pressure to stand out, get people to buy, and get results that can be measured. I wanted to make a resource that takes the mystery out of this process by not only explaining the ideas behind good advertising but also giving useful, doable advice. I want this book to help people who want to push the limits of what's possible in modern ads and also give them ideas.

This book is mostly about more than just making ads that work. Being able to connect with others in a real, artistic, and useful way is what it's all about. If you're new to marketing or just want to improve your current plans, I hope these ideas encourage you to think outside the box, take risks, and make campaigns that not only meet but also exceed standards.

Introduction: Ads That Sell in the Digital Age

"Advertising in the digital age has moved from mass marketing to massive personalization."

– Terence Kawaja

The last ten years have seen a big change in advertising. Campaigns used to be very simple and one-dimensional, but now advertising is a complex field that combines imagination, technology, and data-driven strategy. Consumers today are smarter, more connected, and pickier than ever before, making it harder for marketers to get their products noticed. Traditional methods, such as TV ads, paper ads, and early internet banners, have been supplemented and, in some cases, replaced by a wide range of new channels and formats. Social media sites, search engines, and automated advertising have revolutionized the way ads are delivered, thought about, and measured.

In this new environment, the balance of power has shifted from the marketer to the customer. With very little exertion, a potential buyer can learn all they need to know about your product, read reviews, compare pricing, and make a purchase—skipping all the well-considered messages used to lead them through the marketing funnel. The distribution of information to more people means that ads have to work harder to attract and convince smart people to act. They have to be relevant and up-to-date, and most importantly, they have to hit home deeply.

This book talks about the problems that come up in today's business world. This book is not only a guide for making ads, but also a plan for learning the art and science of marketing in a time when rules are always being changed. This book will give new marketers and experienced marketers who want to improve their skills as well as newcomers who want to make a name for themselves important tools, ideas, and methods for success.

THE NEED FOR UNCONVENTIONAL STRATEGIES

As a Performance Marketing Executive, it was my job to achieve exceptional results and go above and beyond what was expected. That's where the ideas for this book came from. I had to look into unconventional strategies in order to beat rivals, make the most of budgets, and get a measurable return on investment (ROI). Understanding the strategies that used to guarantee success—using broad demographic targets, sending generic messages, and sticking to well-known platforms—didn't take long. But they weren't enough anymore. As the market changed, so did the types of people who bought things.

It became clear that I needed to think about more than what was obvious if I wanted to be successful. I started trying new things, like getting better at copywriting and adding storytelling elements to my ads. Within three months, my clients' sales went up by 50%, thanks to me using new technologies, learning more about data analytics, and, most importantly, encouraging creativity that went beyond the limits of traditional advertising. Because of these tests, campaigns not only worked better, but they also hit home with their target groups more deeply. When I realized that in today's advertising world, it's not enough to just do well within the current framework; you have to change the framework itself.

This book is the result of all those things. It's a collection of techniques, thoughts, and lessons learned over many years of working in the ever-changing world of digital marketing. It is my intention to share in this paper some unconventional strategies that have been shown to work and are based on real-life examples. This book has techniques that will help you reach and even go beyond your goals, even if you have a small budget, a tough target market, or you need to stand out in a crowded market.

WHAT MAKES THIS BOOK UNIQUE?

"Never stop testing, and your advertising will never stop improving."

– David Ogilvy, Founder,
Ogilvy & Mather Advertising Agency

There are many books about advertising, and each one gives a different view on how to make efforts that work. Some focus on the artistic side, others on the technical side, and many try to find a middle ground between the two. This book stands out because it focuses on how to use successful strategies in the real world, adapting them to the specific problems that businesses face today.

The saying "think outside the box" is more important than ever in a world where people get thousands of texts every day. When you think creatively, you think about purposeful uniqueness, not just difference. It means understanding the subtleties of your audience, using facts to make smart decisions, and using creativity to get them emotionally involved.

This book is a how-to guide for marketers who want to make things possible in new ways. It's more than just making ads; it's also about creating experiences that connect, motivate, and call people to action. The answers given here are not theoretical ideas; they are tried-and-true strategies that have been shown to work in real life. They are designed to be flexible so that they can be changed to fit your needs and circumstances. We developed them by reading numerous research papers, observing current consumer and industry trends on social media and in the news, leveraging personal experiences, and examining the work of renowned consumer psychologists. By the end of this book, you'll have a collection of ideas for how to make campaigns that work and people will remember.

A PERSONAL JOURNEY OF LEARNING AND GROWTH

Writing this book has been one of the most personal things I've ever done. This has given me a chance to think about the lessons I've learned at work and to put together the most important ones in a way that can help other people. I started working in digital marketing more than seven years ago, during a time when the field was growing quickly. In the beginning, I was amazed by how digital media could involve large groups of people in a responsible and measurable way.

My role as a Senior Media Buyer in performance marketing agency Clicks Bazaar Technologies, gave me the opportunity to work on a wide range of projects across various industries. Each project brought its own set of challenges, and with each challenge came the opportunity to learn and grow. Over the years, I got better at things like media buying on Facebook, improving e-commerce, and content strategy, while putting innovation and impact first. Being an entrepreneur and media buyer helped me learn more about what it takes to be successful in this dynamic and quickly changing field. It taught me how important it is to be strong, flexible, and able to think creatively when things get tough.

This book is a summary of that journey. It's not just a list of strategies and methods; it's a testament to how important it is to keep learning, trying new things, and being flexible. The world of marketing is always shifting, and the only way to stay ahead of the competition is to change with it. By sharing my thoughts and experiences, I hope to help others easily and creatively navigate this complicated and changing field.

WHAT YOU'LL TAKE AWAY FROM THIS BOOK

This book is full of useful information and ideas that will help you be successful in modern advertising that you can use right away in your campaigns, whether you want to improve the ones you already have or try out some new ones.

Through this book, you will learn how to use AI to expand your imagination, analyze data to make smart choices, and write messages that connect with your audience. In a world where change is the sole constant, you will learn the significance of adaptability and flexibility. Additionally, they will provide you with the necessary tools and mindset to excel in the highly competitive digital marketing industry.

This book is more than just a guide; it's a resource that you can return to again and again as you navigate the challenges and opportunities of modern advertising. My hope is that it will inspire you to think differently, to push the boundaries of what's possible, and to create campaigns that don't just meet the status quo but set new standards for success.

Introduction: Ads That Sell in the Digital Age

"Good marketing makes the company look smart. Great marketing makes the customer feel smart."

– Joe Chernov

THE SECRET SAUCE OF HIGH-CONVERSION ADS

What does it take to make an ad that not only gets people's attention but also gets them to buy something in this modern age? Creative thinking, headlines containing facts or statistics, and a deep understanding of how people act as customers are the keys to finding the answer.

To put it simply, high-conversion advertising is all about impact. Advertisements that get people to buy something do so by directly addressing their wants, needs, and problematic areas. Their purpose is to solve a problem, satisfy a desire, or evoke a feeling, like happiness, fear, nostalgia, or hope. The emotional impact of these ads is backed up by data that makes sure the message is engaging and useful to the audience.

1. **Emotional Connection:** Motivating people with emotions is very effective. Buying choices are often based on how someone feels, and then those feelings are defended with logic. Advertisements that work appeal to these feelings, like the joy of a family dinner, the thrill of a journey, or the relief of solving a problem. Highly effective ads know how to make people feel the right way so that the experience is remembered.
2. **Clarity and Empathy:** In a world full of data, simplicity sticks out. Clearly worded ads with a simple call to action are more likely to get people to act. What is being given, why it matters to them, and what they need to do next should all be clear to consumers right away. Clear layouts, big headlines, and pictures that catch and hold people's attention are all parts of simple design.
3. **Personalization and ease of use:** It's not okay to send boring texts anymore. Ads that get more people to buy are customized to their interests, habits, and groups. To learn a lot about the public, people often use data analysis,

segmentation, and targeting. Personalization is more than just using a customer's name. It also means giving them information that feels like it was made just for them based on their journey and tastes.

4. **Using Several Channels:** Customers today interact with brands in a lot of different ways, such as through social media, websites, emails, and even shops. Because of this, high-conversion ads use campaigns that send the same message through all platforms. To make the brand experience smooth, it doesn't matter where or how a customer sees the ad.
5. **Decisions Based on Data:** A lot of data is used to create a great ad. Data is what makes A/B testing and performance analytics possible. It tells advertisers about their viewers and market trends. It helps us be more creative, improves the effectiveness of our marketing, and gives us concrete results that we can change right away. Business use data to learn what works and what doesn't, as well as how to get better.

People are becoming more wary of ads that seem dishonest or try to trick them when it comes to faith and honesty. People will trust ads that are real and honest more. Real-life stories that connect with what the customer wants and believe in show what the brand stands for. Big brands today don't just sell things; they also bring people together to work toward the same goals.

WHAT THIS BOOK WILL TEACH YOU:

This book is intended to be a thorough resource for navigating the ever-changing world of digital advertising. It will give you a road map for generating ads that not only attract attention but also promote real engagement and conversions. Here's what you'll learn:

Understanding Modern Consumers: The book begins by looking into the attitude of today's consumer. You'll discover the psychological triggers that influence purchasing decisions, how digital habits are changing the marketing funnel, and why knowing consumer intent is more crucial than ever. The first chapters will assist you in understanding consumer behavior, allowing you to build more targeted and effective marketing.

Mastering Emotional Resonance: Learn how to create advertising that has an emotional impact on your target demographic. We'll look at the basic emotions that drive customer behavior—such as fear, joy, wrath, and desire—and show real-world examples of advertising that have successfully tapped into these emotions. This section will help you grasp the importance of empathy and storytelling in developing deep, emotional relationships with your audience.

Harnessing the Power of Simplicity: Find out why less is frequently more in advertising. The book will teach you how to write clear, short messages that cut through the clutter and have a lasting impact. You'll discover the fundamentals of minimalist design, how to write memorable slogans, and see examples of firms that have perfected the art of simplicity.

Visual Impact: In the digital age, graphics are more important than ever. This book will show you how to employ design concepts to catch attention in seconds, the science of first impressions, and the most recent visual trends dominating today's advertising environment. You'll learn how to design images that not only capture attention but also reinforce your brand's message.

The Art of Storytelling: Learn about "storyselling" by looking beyond traditional storytelling. This book will teach you how to write fascinating narratives that not only engage, but also generate purchases. You'll learn about the importance of relatability and authenticity, as well as how to smoothly incorporate your brand's value proposition into the story.

Choosing the Right Channels: Not all platforms are equal. This book will walk you through the process of determining the most effective channels for your campaigns, whether they be Meta, LinkedIn, Google, or elsewhere. You'll learn how to use platform-specific strategies as well as how to make sure your messages are consistent across multiple media to reach more people and have a bigger impact.

Making Irresistible CTAs: Every great ad ends with an appealing call to action. You will learn about the psychology behind good CTAs, how to try and improve them, and see examples of CTAs that get people to take action.

Embracing creativity that is driven by data: Find out how to use facts and creativity together. This part will show you how to use analytics to make your ad campaigns better, avoid relying too much on data, and make changes in real time to make sure your ads are always working at their best.

Navigating Ethics and Authenticity: Discover how to tread the narrow line between persuasion and manipulation. You'll learn the value of transparency, how to develop trust with your target audience, and explore instances of brands that have effectively linked with social causes to improve their image.

Future-Proofing Your Strategy: Finally, the book will provide you with the tools you need to keep ahead of trends. You'll learn about the most recent breakthroughs in AI, augmented reality, and customization, as well as how to adapt to shifting customer behaviors without sacrificing your brand's identity. This part will discuss what's next in advertising and how to future-proof your strategy for long-term success.

CONCLUSION: YOUR JOURNEY BEGINS HERE

For marketers, the digital era presents both an opportunity and a challenge. Regulations are subject to constant change; therefore, in order to succeed, you must be flexible, inventive, and constantly one step ahead. If you read this book, you will have the confidence, creativity, and strategic thinking necessary to navigate this new world.

Chapter 1

Cracking the Consumer Code

"The customer is not a moron; she is your wife."

– David Ogilvy

UNDERSTANDING THE MODERN CONSUMER

The present buyer is somewhat different from the one of the past. Consumers are more knowledgeable, more empowered, and more discriminating than ever before in a time when knowledge is at their fingertips. Gone are the days when one-way channels of communication allowed brands to control consumer behavior. Consumers today have the power; they demand brands to fit them on their terms—that is, whether that means providing transparency, customizing experiences, or matching with their values.

Starting with the elements influencing the behavior of the current consumer helps one to really grasp them. The emergence of digital media has changed everything since it gives consumers quick access to reviews, comparisons, and knowledge. Social media channels have given people a voice, so they may demand responsibility from companies and influence others. As cellphones proliferate, consumers are continuously connected, making real-time purchase decisions and expecting instantaneous company reactions.

THE SHIFT IN CONSUMER EXPECTATIONS

Changing these things has changed consumer expectations. Personalizing is not a luxury anymore; it is a need. Customers want firms to be aware of their tastes, foresight, and demands and to produce pertinent material. There is a drawback to this expectation though—privacy issues. Consumers value tailored experiences, but they are also more conscious of data privacy concerns and wary of how their information is being utilized. For marketers who have to negotiate the thin line separating personalization from privacy, this produces a precarious balance.

The modern customer also prizes openness and honesty. They are curious about the brand's history, ideals, and influence on society, as well as about Companies considered genuine and socially conscious, which usually develop closer relationships with their customers. Conversely, people who come out as dishonest or out of touch could rapidly lose credibility and confidence.

PSYCHOLOGICAL TRIGGERS IN CONSUMER BEHAVIOR

1. Knowing the psychological triggers that affect customer behavior is important for making advertising strategies that work. These causes have been studied for a long time, but their importance in the digital age calls for a new point of view. Here are some of the most important psychological factors to think about:
2. People buy things based on what other people say and do. This is called "social proof." Because of this, reviews, testimonials, and user-generated material are very powerful. People are more likely to buy a product or service from a brand if they know that other people have liked it.
3. Scarcity: The fear of missing out (FOMO) is a very strong motivator. Low stock alerts, special deals, and offers that are only good for a short time can make customers feel rushed and encourage them to act quickly.
4. People who are kind to us feel like they owe it to them to be kind to someone else. This idea is called reciprocity. This can be used in marketing by giving away free trials, freebies, or useful materials to build trust and encourage people to buy again.
5. People often make decisions based on the first piece of information they find, which is called an "anchor." This is why pricing strategies like showing the full price next to the reduced price may work so well. The first price helps to

ground the lower price, making the lower price look like a great deal.

6. People are more likely to trust and do what an expert or powerful person says. This is why endorsements from experts in the field, celebrities, or people with a lot of impact can be very powerful.

BUILDING CONSUMER PERSONAS

To effectively target the diverse consumer segments, it's crucial to develop detailed consumer personas. These personas are fictional representations of your ideal customers, based on real data and insights. A well-crafted persona goes beyond basic demographic information to include psychographic details such as values, interests, pain points, and buying behaviors.

The process of building consumer personas involves several steps:

1. **Collect Data:** Commence by collecting data from diverse sources, encompassing website analytics, social media insights, customer surveys, and market research reports. This information will facilitate your comprehension of customer and brand interactions.
2. **Identify Patterns:** Look for patterns and trends in the data that can help you segment your audience into different groups. For example, you might notice that one segment is highly price-sensitive, while another is more focused on quality and brand reputation.
3. **Create Detailed Profiles:** Develop a comprehensive profile for each group that encompasses demographic data (age, gender, income level), psychographic data (values, hobbies, lifestyle), and behavioral data (buying behaviors, brand loyalty, online behavior).

4. **Name and Optimize Your Personas:** Give each persona a name and a backstory to make them feel more real. For example, "Budget-Conscious Shaba" could be a 35-year-old mom of two who shops for the best deals and values practicality over luxury.

6. **Use Personas in your Performance Marketing Campaign:** Use your personas in your marketing campaign; also personalize your messaging, materials, and campaigns to fit the particular needs and tastes of every persona.

THE ROLE OF DATA IN UNDERSTANDING CONSUMERS

Data is the most important thing for understanding the current consumer. Today, almost every interaction a customer has with a business creates data. This includes clicking on an ad, buying something, and even just interacting with content on social media. This knowledge can help you understand how customers act, what they like, and why they do what they do.

But numbers alone are not enough. Brands need to be able to look at this info and act on it in order to really understand their customers. To do this, you need the right skills and tools to look at data, find patterns, and turn insights into useful answers. More and more, advanced analytics, AI, and machine learning are being used to make sense of very large datasets and give customers more personalized and relevant experiences.

Also, it's important to remember that data should only be used in an honest way. More and more people are aware of how their personal information is being used. Businesses that misuse or abuse this information could lose customers and damage their image. To build long-term relationships with customers, you need to be honest with your facts and be committed to giving them value.

LEVERAGING TECHNOLOGY TO CONNECT WITH CONSUMERS

Technology has revolutionized the way brands connect with consumers. From AI-powered chatbots that provide instant customer service to personalized email campaigns that speak directly to individual preferences, technology enables brands to create more meaningful and engaging interactions with consumers.

Social media platforms, in particular, have become powerful tools for connecting with consumers on a personal level. Platforms like Facebook, Instagram, and Twitter allow brands to engage with their audience in real-time, respond to feedback, and build a community around their brand. Social listening tools can also be used to monitor conversations and trends, providing valuable insights into consumer sentiment and emerging opportunities.

In addition to social media, other technologies such as augmented reality (AR), virtual reality (VR), and voice search are opening up new possibilities for engaging with consumers. For example, AR can be used to create immersive shopping experiences, allowing consumers to virtually try on products before making a purchase. VR can be used to create interactive brand experiences, and voice search optimization can help brands reach consumers who use voice-activated devices like Amazon Echo or Google Home.

THE IMPORTANCE OF EMOTIONAL CONNECTION

Although modern marketing depends much on data and technology, they are insufficient on their own. Emotions drive consumers at the end of the day, hence brands that can emotionally connect with them are more likely to flourish. Beyond just delivering a message, emotional connection is about designing events that appeal to consumers and help them to feel appreciated, understood, and motivated.

"Caretaking and pragmatic support come naturally when we feel close and connected. 'When you love, you wish to do things for."

– Ernest Hemingway

An emotional connection with customers can be developed in a number of ways like:

1. **Storytelling**: Try to use storytelling 90% of the time to convey your brand's values, mission, and personality. Stories have the power to evoke emotions and create a sense of connection with your audience.
2. **Authenticity**: Be genuine, raw, and transparent in your communication. Consumers can easily spot insincerity, and brands that come across as inauthentic will struggle to build trust.
3. **Empathy**: Show empathy by understanding and addressing the needs, concerns, and pain points of your audience. This can be achieved through personalized messaging, responsive customer service, and a commitment to social responsibility.
4. **Consistency**: Make sure that your brand's messaging and values are consistent across all channels and touchpoints. Consistency helps build trust and reinforces the emotional connection with your audience.

ADAPTING TO CONSUMER TRENDS

Today's consumer is constantly evolving, and brands must be able to adapt to changing trends and preferences. Staying ahead of consumer trends requires a combination of data analysis, market research, and a willingness to experiment and innovate.

Some key consumer trends to watch include:

1. **Sustainability**: Consumers are increasingly concerned about environmental and social issues, and they expect brands to take a stand on these matters. Brands that prioritize sustainability and ethical practices are more likely to win the loyalty of socially conscious consumers.

2. **Convenience**: In a fast-paced world, convenience is king. Consumers want products and services that make their lives easier, whether that means faster delivery, simplified checkout processes, or seamless integration with other devices and platforms.

3. **Experience over Products**: Many consumers, especially younger generations, are prioritizing experiences over material possessions. Brands that can create memorable experiences with the brand, whether through events, content, or customer service, will have a competitive edge.

4. **Personalization**: As mentioned earlier, personalization remains a key trend, but it's evolving. Consumers now expect hyperpersonalized experiences that cater to their unique preferences and needs. This requires brands to go beyond basic segmentation and use advanced data analytics to deliver truly individualized content.

CONCLUSION: CRACKING THE CODE

Cracking the consumer code is an ongoing process that requires a deep understanding of who your customers are, what they want, and how they make decisions. It combines psychological knowledge, data-driven insights, and a dedication to provide value via unique, real-life events with a personal resonance.

Using the techniques and tools that have been shown to be successful in the complicated and competitive environment of today, you will learn as you advance in this book how to apply these ideas in your advertising efforts. By the conclusion of this road, you will have the tools and knowledge to not only reach but also interact with your audience in a way that fosters ongoing loyalty and corporate success.

Chapter 2

Emotional Resonance: The Heart of Effective Ads

"I've learned that people will forget what you said, people will forget what you did, but people will never forget how you made them feel."

– Maya Angelou

INTRODUCTION: THE POWER OF EMOTIONAL ADVERTISING

Good advertising revolves mostly around emotional resonance. Emotional advertising offers a means to really and meaningfully engage an audience at a time when consumers are bombarded with knowledge. Emotions clearly affect consumer behavior, decision-making, and brand loyalty according to research. Advertisers may design unforgettable campaigns that not only grab attention but also inspire action and increase interaction by appealing to emotions.

This chapter looks at the psychological foundations of emotional advertising, the several emotions that can be used, and doable techniques for using emotional resonance in your campaigns. Combining knowledge from psychology, marketing theory, and research, we explore how to create ads your audience will find more meaningful.

1. THE PSYCHOLOGICAL BASIS OF EMOTIONAL ADVERTISING

Emotional advertising is based on the way our brains naturally react to things that make us feel strong emotions. Emotions are controlled by the limbic system, a complex group of brain regions that affects behavior, long-term memory, and desire. How we feel affects how we see the world, what choices we make, and how we connect with other people.

DUAL-PROCESS THEORY IN DECISION MAKING

Developed by psychologists including Daniel Kahneman and Amos Tversky, the Dual-Process Theory is one of the fundamental hypotheses explaining why emotions are strong in advertising.

According to this view, the brain consists of two systems used to guide decisions:

System 1: quick, emotional, automatic. Operating automatically, this system regulates gut reactions and natural judgments.

System 2: purposeful, slow, rational. This system is in charge of analytical thinking and logical decision-making as well as of demanding conscious effort.

Emotional advertising largely stimulates System 1, which helps businesses to bypass the more important and doubtful processes of System 2. Ads may start by appealing to emotions, which then prompt immediate responses and influence decisions in a way that rational arguments alone cannot.

THE ROLE OF EMOTIONS IN MEMORY AND RECALL

Making and remembering memories depends much on emotions as well. Cognitive psychology studies such as those by Elizabeth Loftus and others have found that we retain emotionally charged experiences more precisely and deeply than we do of neutral events. This is true since the amygdala serves to store emotional memories and is a fundamental component of the brain's emotional processing system. In advertising, this implies that memories of powerful feeling advertisements are more likely. Emotional resonance is thus a great approach to persuading consumers to recall a brand.

2. TYPES OF EMOTIONS THAT DRIVE CONSUMER BEHAVIOR

When it comes to ads, not all emotions are the same. Emotions can be used to achieve a range of objectives, from getting people to act right away to building brand loyalty over time. Based on research in psychology and business theory, here are some of the main types of emotions and how they affect how people act:

a. Fear → feeling of being afraid, frightened, or scared.

b. Anger → feeling angry. A stronger word for anger is rage.

c. Sadness → feeling sad. Other words are sorrow, grief (a stronger feeling, for example, when someone has died).

d. Joy → the inward feeling of happiness that exists no matter the circumstance, whether good or bad.

e. Disgust → feeling something is wrong or nasty. Strong disapproval.

f. Surprise → being unprepared for something.

g. Trust → a positive emotion; admiration is stronger; acceptance is weaker.

h. Anticipation → in the sense of looking forward positively to something that is going to happen. Expectation is more neutral.

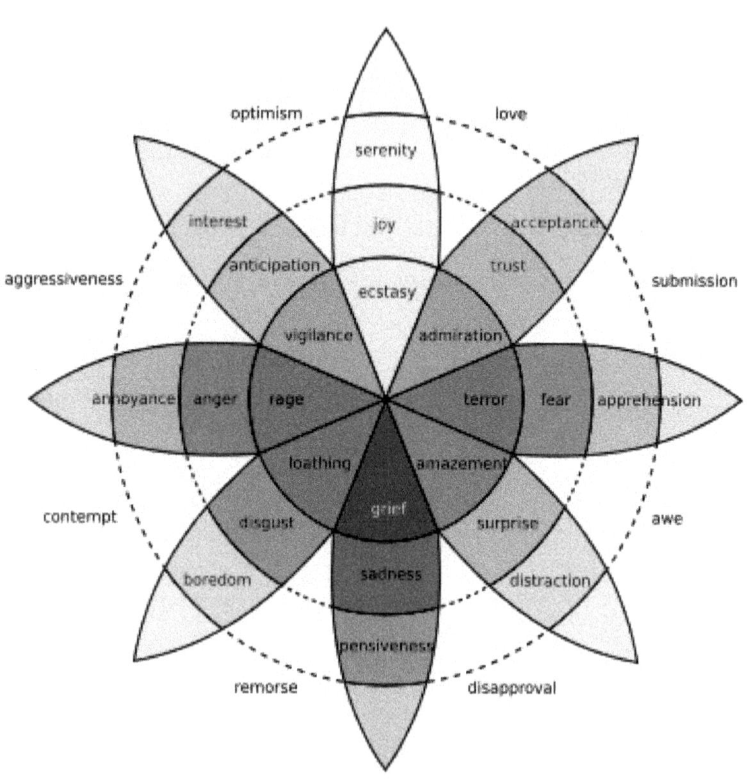
optimism
love
serenity
interest
joy
acceptance
anticipation
trust
aggressiveness
submission
ecstasy
vigilance
admiration
annoyance
anger
rage
terror
fear
apprehension
loathing
amazement
contempt
grief
awe
disgust
surprise
boredom
sadness
distraction
pensiveness
remorse
disapproval

- **Positive Emotions (Joy, Love, Surprise):** Positive emotions are often used to create a favorable association with a brand. Research by Barbara Fredrickson on the "Broaden-and-Build Theory" suggests that positive emotions broaden our attention and thinking, making us more receptive to new experiences and more likely to engage in creative problem-solving. In advertising, this translates to higher engagement and shareability of content that makes people feel good.
- **Negative Emotions (Fear, Sadness, Anger):** While less frequently used, negative emotions can be powerful motivators when applied correctly. Studies such as those by Paul Ekman on basic emotions indicate that emotions like fear and anger can prompt immediate action, such as making a purchase to avoid a perceived threat. Fear appeals, for example, are often used in health campaigns to encourage preventive behavior by highlighting potential risks.
- **Mixed Emotions (Nostalgia, Bittersweet):** Mixed emotions, which combine positive and negative feelings, can create a complex and memorable experience for the audience. Research by psychologists like Constantine Sedikides has shown that nostalgia, for instance, can increase consumers' willingness to pay for products by evoking a sense of comfort and a connection to the past. Bittersweet emotions can also foster deep reflection and a stronger emotional bond with the message.

3. THE ROLE OF EMPATHY AND EMOTIONAL CONTAGION

Empathy is the ability to understand and share the feelings of others. In advertising, empathetic messages can create a sense of connection and relatability that resonates deeply with the audience. Empathy taps into a human's innate social nature and desire for connection, making it a powerful tool for building brand loyalty.

THEORY OF MIND AND EMPATHY IN ADVERTISING

Theory of Mind (ToM) refers to the ability to attribute mental states—beliefs, intents, desires, emotions—to oneself and others. This cognitive skill allows humans to predict and interpret the behavior of others, making it essential for social interactions. In advertising, messages that effectively use ToM can guide the audience to see themselves in the narrative, enhancing empathy and connection.

Research by Simon Baron-Cohen and other cognitive scientists has highlighted that empathetic messaging works particularly well in storytelling formats, where audiences can see the world through another person's perspective. By creating characters and scenarios that reflect the audience's experiences, advertisers can build a strong empathetic response.

EMOTIONAL CONTAGION THEORY

Emotional Contagion Theory, developed by researchers like Elaine Hatfield, John Cacioppo, and Richard Rapson, describes the phenomenon where individuals "catch" emotions from others. In advertising, this means that the emotions displayed in ads can be transferred to viewers, making them feel what the characters in the ad feel. This can be especially powerful in video and audio formats, where facial expressions, tone of voice, and music can all contribute to the spread of emotion.

4. STRATEGIES FOR CREATING EMOTIONALLY RESONANT ADS

Crafting ads that resonate emotionally with the audience involves strategic planning and a deep understanding of your target demographic. Below are key strategies grounded in psychological principles and marketing theory:

A. Take advantage of emotional archetypes

Archetypes are characters or symbols that everyone knows and that make us think of certain feelings and stories. Carl Jung was a psychologist who found archetypes that are strongly rooted in all cultures. Some examples are the Hero, the Caregiver, and the Rebel. In ads, these characters can be used to quickly get across complicated thoughts and feelings. For example, using a Hero archetype can make you feel brave and ready for adventure, while using a Caregiver archetype can make you feel safe and cared for.

B. Tell stories that people can relate to and are true.

In emotional ads, being real is very important. Jennifer Aaker and others at Stanford University have done research that shows stories that feel real and relevant are more convincing and lasting. To do this, ads should show things that really happen, raw ads yield better results, use everyday & easy words, and stay away from showing things that are too perfect or not realistic. Real stories not only build trust, but they also help people see themselves in the ad, which makes them more emotionally invested.

C. Add visual and auditory elements to make emotions stronger

Visuals and sounds are very important for understanding emotions. Music and feeling studies by people like Daniel Levitin have shown that different kinds of music can make people feel different emotions, like happiness, sadness, or nostalgia. When performance marketing ads use the right mix of colors, sounds, and pictures, they can make people feel stronger about what they see or hear.

Cooler colors, like blue and green, can calm you down and make you believe others. Warmer colors, like red and yellow, can get you moving and excited.

D. Write down your mental highs and lows.

The Nobel Prize winner Daniel Kahneman studied the Peak-End Rule, which says that people mostly judge events by how they made them feel at the start and end. For ads, this means that adding emotional peaks (moments of high energy) and a strong, positive ending can make the whole thing much more powerful. Making a strong finish that people will remember and a thrilling climax can have an effect that lasts.

E. Align Emotions with Brand Values and purposes

Emotional resonance is most effective when it aligns with the brand's core values and purpose. Antonio Lucio has advocated for purpose-driven advertising, where emotional appeals are not just tactics but are deeply rooted in the brand's mission. Ads that evoke emotions related to the brand's values—such as sustainability, innovation, or community—can build a more coherent and compelling brand narrative, leading to stronger customer loyalty.

F. Use Social Proof and Emotional Contagion

Social proof, a concept popularized by psychologist Robert Cialdini, involves leveraging the behavior of others to influence decision-making. Ads that show positive emotional reactions from real customers, testimonials, or influencer endorsements can trigger emotional contagion, where viewers adopt the same feelings. This strategy can be particularly effective in digital and social media, where user-generated content and peer recommendations carry significant weight.

5. FIGURING OUT HOW WELL EMOTIONAL MARKETING WORKS

There are more than just click-through and view rates that can be used to judge how well emotional ads work. Think about the following ways of judging to fully understand how important the emotional link is:

A. Paying attention to how people feel

As neuromarketing has grown, new ways to track how people feel have become possible, such as EEG (electroencephalography), face coding, and galvanic skin reactions.

B. Sentiment Analysis on Social Media

When people talk about and react to ads on social media, sentiment analysis tools can track and rate how people feel about them. Marketers can figure out how an ad makes people feel by listening to what they have to say about it. They change how they do things to fit after that.

C. Loyalty to the brand and repeat business over time

When people have a personal connection with a business, they are more likely to stick with it. To get a better idea of how emotional advertising changes people's long-term decisions, you can keep an eye on things like customer lifetime value, brand support, and return buy rates.

D. Polls and meetings with groups

Focus groups and surveys give you straight answers about how an ad makes people feel. You can learn how to make better emotional calls in the future by listening to people talk about how they felt and how that changed how they saw the brand.

CONCLUSION: HARNESSING THE POWER OF EMOTIONS IN ADVERTISING

Emotional resonance is a key method for creating meaningful and memorable advertising. Advertisers may make significant connections with their audience by understanding the psychological principles underlying emotions, using storytelling and visual aspects, and matching emotional appeals with brand values. As the advertising landscape evolves, the ability to elicit genuine emotions will remain a critical difference for organizations looking to stand out and develop long-term relationships with their customers.

This upcoming chapter uses a range of psychology research and marketing theory to give a complete look at how to use emotional resonance in advertising. Media buyers can make ads that not only get people's attention but also get them to act and build loyalty by combining these facts and techniques.

Chapter 3

The Power of Simplicity – Less Is More in Performance Marketing

"The best marketing doesn't feel like marketing."

– Tom Fishburne

INTRODUCTION: WHY SIMPLICITY MATTERS IN PERFORMANCE MARKETING

In the fast-paced digital world, consumers are faced with an overwhelming amount of information, data, and options. For brands to capture attention and drive measurable actions, simplicity has become a vital strategy, particularly in performance marketing. Performance marketing focuses on tangible outcomes—whether it's generating leads, increasing conversions, or maximizing return on investment (ROI). Simplifying your message and design can guide users seamlessly through the conversion funnel, reduce friction, and ultimately drive results.

Simplicity in performance marketing means more than just clean visuals; it's about delivering concise, focused messaging and optimizing every touchpoint in the customer journey to improve conversion rates. In this chapter, we'll explore how simplicity enhances performance marketing strategies and showcase real-world examples where a minimalist approach has led to measurable success.

THE SCIENCE OF SIMPLICITY IN PERFORMANCE MARKETING

The brain is naturally set up to like things that are easy. People can experience cognitive overload when they have too many options or too much complicated knowledge. This can make them unable to decide or lose interest. For performance marketers, lowering brain load is key to making quick decisions and taking action right away. A simple, focused approach makes sure that users aren't swamped and can easily figure out what to do, whether it's through ads, landing pages, or email campaigns.

1. **Clarity Makes Things Smoother**: A short, clear message that tells users directly what the value proposition is lowers

the barriers that might stop them from converting. Users should know right away what the deal is and what they need to do next.

2. **Conversion is Driven by Memorable Simplicity**: Performance marketing that is kept simple makes the message more powerful, which makes it easier for users to remember and act on. A simple, well-designed ad can stay in people's minds, which makes it more likely that they will convert later.
3. **Keeping things simple makes them more effective**: projects with fewer moving parts are easier to test, analyze, and improve. This lets changes happen more quickly and based on data, which leads to better marketing performance and a higher return on investment (ROI).

HOW SIMPLICITY ENHANCES USER EXPERIENCE AND CONVERSION RATES

In performance marketing, user experience (UX) is directly tied to conversion rates. Simplicity plays a key role in optimizing UX by removing unnecessary distractions and guiding users toward a single, clear action.

Here are a few critical ways that simplicity improves UX and drives conversions:

1. **Streamlined User Journey**: Every step in the user journey—from ad click to landing page to checkout—should be streamlined. By reducing unnecessary steps, options, or distractions, you make it easier for users to move through the funnel without getting sidetracked or confused.
2. **Faster Load Times**: Minimalist designs and lean content ensure fast-loading ads and landing pages. In performance

marketing, page speed is crucial: slower pages lead to higher bounce rates and lower conversion rates. Simplicity ensures that your assets load quickly, keeping users engaged and more likely to complete the desired action.

3. **Focused Call to Action (CTA)**: A well-placed, action-oriented CTA is essential in performance marketing. Simplicity ensures that the CTA stands out and guides users to take the next step, whether it's signing up, making a purchase, or downloading content.

EXAMPLES FROM REAL LIFE OF HOW SIMPLICITY CAN DRIVE RESULTS IN PERFORMANCE MARKETING

A number of well-known brands have used simplicity in their performance marketing campaigns, showing that going with a simple method can yield excellent results:

1. Early Advertising for Dropbox

When Dropbox first started out, their landing pages were very simple. They had very little writing, one video that explained the product, and a clear call to action that said, "Sign Up for Free." This method got rid of any extraneous distractions and focused only on getting people to sign up, and it worked. Dropbox grew very quickly because their deal was clear and simple to take advantage of.

2. How Easy Google Ads Is for High Conversion

People like how simple Google's paid search ads are. There is writing in each ad, with a clear headline, a short description, and a strong call to action (CTA) like "Buy Now" or "Get a Quote." This simple layout helps people find what they need and act quickly, which makes Google Ads one of the best performance marketing tools for click-through rates and conversions.

3. Shopify's offer of a free trial

Shopify's free trial ads show that keeping things simple can lead to more sales. They usually use a clean style and a simple message in their ads: "Start your free trial today." By focusing on this one deal and getting rid of any other options, Shopify gets thousands of business owners who want to try out the platform to convert.

4. Amazon's Faster 1-Click Checkout

Amazon's checkout process is very simple, with only a few steps and clear calls to action (CTAs). In order to make it easy for people to buy things, Amazon uses techniques like one-click buying and a clean, easy-to-navigate design. This is a big reason why Amazon has such high conversion rates.

Make your value proposition clearer: Ask yourself: What is the one most important thing that people should get out of this campaign before you start it? Make sure your message is clear and tells people about this benefit right away.

Get Rid of Distractions: Get rid of anything on your ads or landing pages that doesn't help you reach your sales goal. This could have images, links, or words that aren't needed and could confuse or overwhelm users.

Put speed and efficiency first: Make sure that all of your marketing materials load fast, especially on phones and tablets. In performance marketing, it's important that ads and pages run quickly so that users have a better experience and don't leave the site right away.

Pick out one CTA: Pay attention to one clear CTA per asset, whether you want people to sign up, buy, or click. It's important that the CTA is easy to see and understand.

FIGURING OUT HOW YOUR COMMUNICATION WORKS PERFORMANCE MARKETING

Keep an eye on these key performance indicators (KPIs) to make sure your simplified ads work:

1. **Rate of Conversion:** Keep an eye on how well your ads and landing pages turn people who click on them into customers or leads.
2. **Click-Through Rate (CTR):** If your CTR is high, it means that your message is likely clear and highly engaging. Ads with high engagement rate and focus on one main message tend to perform better.
3. **Bounce Rate:** If your bounce rate is high, it could mean that your page is too hard to use or that people aren't quickly getting the information they need. Most of the time, simpler patterns get less bounces.
4. **Cost per Conversion (CPC):** Costs per conversion are usually lower when things are kept simple. This is because users are more likely to engage with messages that are clear and to the point.

MAKING YOUR PERFORMANCE MARKETING STRATEGY SIMPLER

Focus on the following steps to successfully add simplicity to your performance marketing campaigns:

1. **Make your value proposition more clear:** Ask yourself before you start a campaign: What is the most important thing that people should get out of it? Make sure that your message is clear and tells people about this benefit right away.

2. **Get rid of distractions:** Get rid of any parts of your ads or landing pages that don't help you reach your sales goal. This could include pictures, links, or words that aren't needed and could confuse or overwhelm users.
3. **Speed and efficiency should come first:** Make sure all of your marketing materials load fast, especially on phones and tablets. It's important for performance marketing that ads and pages run quickly so that users have a better experience and don't leave the site right away.
4. **One call to action should be your main focus:** You should have one clear CTA per item whether you want people to sign up, buy, or click. Make sure that the CTA is easy to read and sticks out.

FINDING OUT WHAT EFFECTS SIMPLICITY HAS ON PERFORMANCE MARKETING

Watch these key performance indicators (KPIs) to make sure your streamlined efforts work:

1. **Rate of conversion**: Watch how well your ads and landing pages turn people who see them into leads or customers.
2. **Rate of Clicks (CTR)**: If your CTR is high, it means that your message is likely clear and appealing. Because they focus on one main action, ads that are simple tend to do better.
3. **Rate of Bounces**: If your bounce rate is high, it could mean that your page is too difficult to understand or that people are having trouble quickly getting the information they need. A lot of the time, simpler patterns get fewer bounces.
4. **Cost Per Conversion (CPC)**: Costs per conversion are usually lower when things are kept simple. This is because

users are more likely to engage with messages that are clear and to the point.

CONCLUSION: WHY SIMPLICITY IS YOUR COMPETITIVE EDGE

In performance marketing, simplicity is more than a stylistic choice—it's a strategy that drives real results. You can get more conversions and make the user experience better by making sure messages are clear, user flows are streamlined, and pages load quickly. There should be no unnecessary information or distractions for users. This will make them more likely to be interested in your offer and take the next step.

Remember that less can be more when you're planning your marketing. To make things easy in performance marketing, keep things simple. To make sure that every interaction has the most impact possible, keep things simple.

Chapter 4

Building a Brand Identity That Sticks

"A brand is the set of expectations, memories, stories, and relationships that, taken together, account for a consumer's decision to choose one product or service over another."

– Seth Godin

INTRODUCTION: THE ESSENCE OF BRAND IDENTITY

The whole picture of a brand that its customers see is its character. In addition to the things that people see, touch, and feel, this includes things that people connect with and relate to the business. In a crowded market, where you need to stand out to get and keep buyers' attention, you need a strong brand personality. Today, we'll look at the most important parts of brand identity with the help of well-known branding and advertising experts like Seth Godin, David Ogilvy, Antonio Lucio, Gary Vaynerchuk, and more.

UNDERSTANDING THE CORE OF BRAND IDENTITY

Brand identity is the sum of all the elements that a company creates to portray the right image to its audience. It includes:

Visual Component: Some of the visual parts of a brand are its name, color scheme, fonts, images, and other design elements that make it easy to recognize and like.

Verbal Components: The speech, tone, and style of messaging that show who the brand is and what it stands for.

Emotional and Experiential Elements: The feelings and experiences that the brand evokes, shaping how it is perceived and remembered by consumers.

DAVID OGILVY'S LEGACY: CONSISTENCY AND CLARITY

He thought that all channels should have the same visual and verbal style, so that every ad would show the brand's core ideals and promise.

Ogilvy's approach emphasized understanding the customer deeply and crafting messages that align with their needs and aspirations. He believed in maintaining a consistent visual and verbal style across all media channels, ensuring that every ad reflected the brand's core values and promise.

THE PILLARS OF BRAND IDENTITY

To make your business stand out, you need to pay attention to a few important things:

1. **Brand's Goals and Purpose:** Figure out why your brand exists and what it wants to do besides make money.
2. **Brand Values:** Establish the principles that guide your brand's actions and decisions. These values should resonate with your target audience and be consistently reflected in your communications.
3. **Visual Identity:** Create a cohesive visual identity that includes logos, color palettes, fonts, and imagery. This should be distinctive and adaptable across various media.
4. **Verbal Identity:** Develop a unique brand voice and tone. Whether your brand is playful, authoritative, or empathetic, this voice should be evident in all written and spoken communications.
5. **What the customer thought:** When people visit your website or call customer service, your company's name should always be clear.

ANTONIO LUCIO'S APPROACH: PURPOSE-DRIVEN BRANDING

Antonio Lucio is a well-known marketing leader who has been the CMO of Facebook, Visa, and HP, among other companies. Branding with a reason is very important to him. He says brands should have a clear goal that isn't just to make money and sell stuff. It seems like these brands would like to improve the world. Lucio was in charge of the "Reinvent Mindsets" program at HP. This campaign was all about being open and accepting to everyone. This campaign was a great fit for HP's values and really spoke to its viewers.

Lucio wants the brand to have a reason in everything it does, from making products to talking about them in ads. This way, the brand's personality isn't just on the outside; it's in its very DNA.

CRAFTING A BRAND IDENTITY WITH A STRONG VISUAL AND VERBAL PRESENCE

It's important for brands to have strong visuals so that people can know and remember them. The name, color scheme, fonts, and pictures you use for your brand should all match. This will give it a uniform look that shows who you are.

Making a mark is important because that's what people think of first when they think of a brand. It must be useful, simple, and easy to remember. The best logos, like the Nike swoosh or Apple's apple, are instantly recognizable and communicate the brand's essence.

1. **Color Palette:** Colors evoke emotions and can significantly impact brand perception. Choose a color palette that aligns with your brand's personality and appeals to your target audience.
2. **Typography:** Fonts are more than just letters; they convey tone and style. Whether you choose a classic serif font for a traditional look or a modern sans-serif for a contemporary feel, your typography should complement your overall brand identity.
3. **Imagery and Graphics:** Use consistent imagery that reflects your brand's values and resonates with your audience.

This includes photographs, illustrations, and other visual elements.

GARY VAYNERCHUK'S INSIGHTS: THE IMPORTANCE OF AUTHENTICITY

Gary Vaynerchuk, a leading entrepreneur and marketing guru, is renowned for his emphasis on authenticity in branding. Vaynerchuk advocates for brands to be transparent, genuine, and true to themselves, which he believes builds stronger connections with consumers. He often highlights the importance of personal branding, where the entrepreneur or spokesperson's own values and voice become integral to the brand identity.

Vaynerchuk's approach involves leveraging social media to humanize the brand, engage directly with customers, and showcase the people behind the brand. This strategy not only enhances authenticity but also fosters a sense of community and loyalty among followers.

THE ROLE OF STORYTELLING IN BRAND IDENTITY

Storytelling is a strong way to make your business stand out in a good way. Brands can talk about their mission, beliefs, and personality in a way that people can understand and remember.

How to Tell a Story About Your Business: Why should people care about your brand? Your brand story should tell them who you are and what you stand for. This story should be a part of everything you do to sell your business, from ads to social media posts.

Emotional Connection: Stories that evoke emotions are more likely to be remembered and shared. Use storytelling to connect with your audience on a deeper level, whether through inspirational tales of your brand's journey or customer success stories.

Consistency Across Channels: Your company story should be the same on all channels and platforms. The narrative that a consumer experiences with your organization should be consistent, regardless of whether they engage with it through a television advertisement, social media, or a customer service call.

Seth Godin's philosophy is as follows: Being remarkable and narrating stories. Seth Godin, a marketing expert, underscores the significance of being remarkable in order to distinguish oneself in a chaotic world. Godin's "Purple Cow" idea pushes brands to be unique in the stories they tell and the products they sell. Brands should try to make stories that people will want to talk about, that they will remember and share, he says.

Godin's way of telling stories is to figure out what makes your brand special and then write stories that show off those unique traits. Focusing on what makes your brand unique will help you build an identity that draws in and keeps customers.

PRACTICAL STEPS FOR BUILDING AND SUSTAINING A STRONG BRAND IDENTITY

Creating a business identity that lasts takes planning and hard work. Here are some useful steps to help you get through the process:

1. **Do an Audit of Your Brand**: Check back often to see how your community sees your brand. To do this, you need to look at your brand's visual character, messaging, and customer experience to make sure they fit with your values and speak to your ideal customers.
2. **Figure out where your brand fits in**: Explain in detail what makes your business different from others on the market. Your business should be positioned in this way in everything, from the way you talk to people to the way your logo looks.

3. **Write down all of your brand's style rules**: For all of your platforms to look the same, you need a brand style guide. And the best ways to use your brand and connect with people. It should also have rules about how to talk and look.
4. **Ask the people there what they need and wan**t. To do this, you can use votes, social media, and just plain words. There are useful things you can learn from this talk that will help you make your brand's personality stronger.
5. **Adapt and change**: If your business brand is strong, you can adapt to new times while staying true to your core values. Change your brand name often to keep it fresh.

REAL-WORLD EXAMPLES OF ENDURING BRAND IDENTITIES

1. **The Ogilvy Approach to Luxury Branding: I**n campaigns for high-end brands, Ogilvy has consistently employed a refined visual style and sophisticated messaging that appeal to affluent consumers. This approach involves meticulous attention to detail, from the choice of typography to the tone of voice, creating an aura of exclusivity and elegance.
2. **Lucio's Work at HP:** Antonio Lucio's efforts to rebrand HP focused on making the company more relevant to younger, more diverse audiences. By emphasizing innovation and inclusivity, Lucio was able to refresh HP's brand identity while retaining the elements that made it a trusted name in technology.
3. **Gary Vaynerchuk's VaynerMedia:** Vaynerchuk's agency, VaynerMedia, has built its identity on the principles of speed, innovation, and client-first service. By staying at the forefront of digital trends and fostering a culture of

creativity, VaynerMedia has positioned itself as a dynamic and forward-thinking player in the advertising world.

4. **Seth Godin's Purple Cow Philosophy:** Godin's work emphasizes the importance of differentiation. When brands take this approach, they often do bold and unusual things with their brand, like making new product lines or advertising campaigns that get people's attention and start a conversation.

FIGURING OUT HOW BRAND IDENTITY WORKS

You should keep an eye on how your brand name works to make sure it works well. There are two types of tests that you can use to see how well your brand personality connects with your audience:

1. **Know your brand:** Keep an eye on brand memory, recognition, and reach to see how well your brand is known among the people you want to reach.
2. **Get consumers to return:** Monitor metrics such as net promoter scores and return buy rates to discover how your brand identity influences long-term customer relationships.
3. **How to Measure Engagement:** Look at engagement to see how many people are interacting with your company through websites, social media, and other channels. A strong and meaningful brand for a firm is frequently an indicator of high engagement.
4. **Analysis of emotions:** Use emotion research methods to monitor how consumers perceive your brand. If consumers are satisfied with your brand, it signifies that it matches what they want and expect.

FUTURE-PROOFING YOUR BRAND IDENTITY

Brands need to be able to change with the times. If you follow these steps, your brand's style will last:

1. **Be open to new ideas**: For your business to stay on top of the game in your field, use new tools and platforms. Such as using virtual reality (AR) for work or checking out new social networking sites.
2. **Adoptability Sustainability**: People are becoming more and more interested in brands that care about the environment and other people. If you want to connect with conscious customers, make these ideas a part of your business.
3. **Learning and adapting all the time**: Make sure that everyone on your brand team always learns new things. Always know what's new in your business, how people act, and how to brand yourself in order to keep your brand personality fresh and up to date.
4. **Spend money on brand loyalty programs**: To build long-lasting connections with your customers, offer them VIP experiences, loyalty programs, and deals that are in line with your brand's values and personality

CONCLUSION: BUILDING A BRAND IDENTITY THAT STANDS THE TEST OF TIME

You can't just build a strong brand personality once. You have to keep learning, changing, and coming up with new ideas. Focus on being consistent, being real, and making an emotional connection. Get ideas from branding greats like David Ogilvy, Antonio Lucio, Gary Vaynerchuk, and Seth Godin to make a brand personality that stands out and lasts.

As a basic business strategy, you should put money into your brand name and keep changing it to fit your audience's changing wants and needs. If you do things right, your brand can be more than just a name or a seal. Customers may think of it as a sign of trust, quality, and worth for a long time.

Chapter 5

Storyselling—Beyond Storytelling

"We are, as a species, addicted to stories.
Even when the body goes to sleep,
the mind stays up all night, telling itself stories."

– Jonathan Gottschall

THE SHIFT FROM STORYTELLING TO STORYSELLING IN PERFORMANCE MARKETING

It used to be that telling stories was a great way to sell, but now it's not enough just to get people's attention. The goal of performance marketing is to get activities that can be measured, such as clicks, sign-ups, and sales. This is where telling stories comes in.

Storyselling moves beyond traditional storytelling by weaving the brand directly into the narrative in a way that pushes the audience towards a clear action. It's not just about telling a good story; it's about using that story to deliver results. Whether it's purchasing a product, filling out a form, or subscribing to a service, storyselling makes the brand central to solving a problem or fulfilling a desire—turning engagement into conversions.

5 REASONS WHY STORYTELLING DRIVE RESULTS

Storyselling works especially well in performance marketing because it gets people to do something instead of just being interested. There is a clear goal behind the story: to change. It's not just there to entertain or educate. It works because of these things:

1. **It's Relatable:** When people can relate to the story, it becomes more engaging. People are more inclined to trust the brand as a solution if they can identify with the story's problem or goal.
2. **Authenticity Equals Trust**: Genuine products are extremely valued by modern consumers. Effective storyselling is about presenting real, honest stories free from forced manipulation. One of the most important conversion elements is trust; this helps create it.
3. **Emotion Fuels Action**: Emotional connections aren't just for branding—they're crucial in performance marketing

too. Whether it's excitement, fear of missing out, or empathy, emotions can drive immediate actions, such as signing up for a trial or making a purchase.

4. **Memorability Drive Conversions**: A story is much easier for people to remember than specifics about a product. When the customer is ready to buy, your product will still be in their thoughts because of the story that connects the brand and the solution.
5. **Boost Urgency**: In performance marketing, urgency can make all the difference between someone showing interest and acting. Storyselling frequently uses urgency to get people to move faster rather than later.

CORE ELEMENTS OF STORYSELLING IN PERFORMANCE MARKETING

To drive performance results, storyselling campaigns need to incorporate key elements that not only engage the audience but move them toward an actionable step.

1. **Clear Brand Integration**: The brand or product must be essential to the resolution of the story. It's not just part of the background but rather the hero that solves the consumer's problem or meets their needs. In storyselling, the product is part of the solution.
2. **Relatable Protagonists**: The characters in the story should reflect the real-life challenges or desires of the target audience. If the viewer can see themselves in the protagonist, they are far more likely to take action and believe in the brand's value.
3. **A Tangible Problem**: Every great story centers on a conflict or problem, but in performance marketing, this problem

should be something the audience experiences and wants to solve. The brand then becomes the clear, accessible solution.

4. **Emotional and Rational Appeal**: Storyselling needs to balance emotional resonance with a logical path to action. While emotions drive engagement, there must be a clear and easy-to-understand reason to convert—be it saving money, improving quality of life, or making a process easier.
5. **Compelling Call to Action (CTA)**: The CTA should be woven into the story naturally. After building up the narrative, there must be a clear, actionable next step—whether it's clicking a link, signing up for a trial, or purchasing a product immediately. It's subtle, but there's no mistaking the purpose: conversion.

REAL-WORLD EXAMPLES OF PERFORMANCE-FOCUSED STORYSELLING

Let's dive into real examples of brands using storyselling in performance marketing to drive concrete, measurable results—whether it's sales, sign-ups, or other conversions.

EXAMPLE 1: PELOTON—"THIS IS HOW YOU PUSH"

- **Overview**: Peloton's performance marketing campaigns are a textbook example of storyselling that drives conversions. The ads show relatable individuals overcoming real challenges—busy schedules, fitness plateaus, or motivation issues—and how Peloton is central to their success.
- **Strategy**: Instead of a generic fitness ad, Peloton taps into the emotional and physical struggles of its audience. The product is presented not just as a tool, but as the solution to getting stronger, healthier, or more motivated. The CTA,

"Get yours today," with a clear option to start a payment plan, makes it easy for the viewer to move from inspiration to action.

- **Results**: The campaign led to a significant rise in subscriptions and sales, with a notable increase in trial sign-ups within days of the ads going live. By focusing on real people and real solutions, Peloton converted storytelling into high-impact sales.

EXAMPLE 2: DOLLAR SHAVE CLUB—"OUR"BLADES ARE F*ING GREAT"**

- **Overview**: Dollar Shave Club's famous ad was more than just entertaining—it was a masterclass in performance marketing. This viral video wasn't about raising awareness alone—it was about driving direct-to-consumer sales.
- **Strategy**: The ad combines humor, relatability, and a very clear value proposition: affordable, high-quality razors delivered to your door. The character (the founder) spoke directly to the frustrations of men fed up with overpriced razors, making Dollar Shave Club the obvious solution. The CTA was simple and to the point: "Join now."
- **Results**: Within 48 hours of the ad launching, Dollar Shave Club received over 12,000 orders. It wasn't just a viral hit; it was a performance marketing triumph that led to massive subscriptions.

EXAMPLE 3: CASPER: "BETTER SLEEP AWAITS"

- **Overview**: Casper's storyselling approach focused on real people who struggled with sleep problems and how their mattress was the simple, affordable solution to better sleep.

- **Strategy**: The campaign didn't just highlight product features—it zeroed in on the experience of bad sleep and how it impacts daily life. Casper framed the mattress as the hero, turning sleepless nights into restful ones. The CTA led directly to a limited-time offer, creating urgency to convert viewers into buyers.
- **Results:** These ads led to a big rise in sales for Casper, especially among first-time buyers who were motivated by their desire for a better night's sleep.

EXAMPLE 4: WARBY PARKER – "THE PERKS OF BUYING GLASSES ONLINE."

- **Overview**: The digital-first method that Warby Parker took changed the way people shop for glasses. In their performance marketing, Warby Parker told the story of people who were stuck in the way they usually bought things and how they could get what they wanted in a better, faster way.
- **Strategy**: The brand's storyselling ads focused on common pain points—expensive glasses, inconvenient in-store fittings—and showed how Warby Parker's online model solved these problems. The CTA was clear: "Try 5 pairs at home for free," which drove traffic straight to their home try-on program.
- **Results**: Warby Parker experienced a massive boost in sign-ups for their try-on service, turning viewers into leads and, ultimately, customers.

HOW TO BUILD YOUR OWN STORYSELLING CAMPAIGN FOR PERFORMANCE

In performance marketing, storytelling campaigns are about crafting a narrative that motivates people to act as much as they are about presenting a decent one. Here is exactly, methodically, how to accomplish it:

1. **Know Your Audience Inside Out**: Knowing your audience's problems, wants, and actions is the first step to telling a good story. Your story needs to be directly about them, showing that you understand what they're going through and placing your brand as the answer.
2. **Position Your Brand as the Solution**: Make sure that the story is about your product or service. The customer must believe that what you're selling will solve their issue. The better, the more easily this fits into the story.
3. **Balance Emotion and Logic**: Get your viewers to feel something, but also give them clear, logical reasons to act. They should feel like they have a connection to the story, and be sure that your goods make sense.
4. **Create a Sense of Urgency**: Urgency is great for performance marketing. To get people to act quickly, use limited-time deals, special offers, or perks that they can get right away.
5. **Make the CTA Effortless**: There shouldn't be any problems getting from the story to the action. Make sure the next step is easy, clear, and doesn't require much work from the customer, whether it's a "Buy Now" button, a link to a landing page, or a straight sign-up form.

CONCLUSION: STORYSELLING FOR PERFORMANCE MARKETING

You need to tell stories in modern performance marketing because they make people feel things and help them see their clear, attainable goal. Setting your brand at the heart of the story and making it look like the answer will help you make more sales, keep customers, and connect with them.

There is a lot of competition on the internet these days. Brands that can tell great stories and use them to get real, observable outcomes will stand out.

Chapter 6

The Medium is the Message—Choosing the Right Channels

"Content marketing is really like a first date.
If all you do is talk about yourself,
there won't be a second date."

– **David Beebe**

INTRODUCTION: THE ROLE OF PLATFORM IN PERFORMANCE MARKETING

In performance marketing, selecting the right platform is critical for hitting your KPIs, whether it's conversions, sign-ups, or purchases. It's not just about the message itself but also *where* you deliver that message. The phrase "the medium is the message" by media theorist Marshall McLuhan rings particularly true in today's marketing landscape. Every platform influences how your audience perceives and reacts to your ad, which directly impacts performance.

Each platform has its own distinct user behavior, ad formats, and opportunities for targeting. A Facebook ad might not be as successful on TikTok. Results on Instagram might not hold true on LinkedIn. Understanding the subtleties of every channel and adjusting your strategy to fit those subtleties will help you to release the greatest results for your performance campaigns. This chapter will assist you in maximizing the possibilities of several platforms to reach your objectives related to performance marketing.

THE POWER OF TAILORED STRATEGIES

A one-size-fits-all approach doesn't work in performance marketing. To get results, you need to tailor your campaigns not only to your audience but to the unique dynamics of each platform. It's essential to understand how users engage with content, what drives action on that platform, and how you can optimize ad formats to maximize ROI.

Let's take a closer look at the major platforms and explore performance-driven strategies for each one.

1. FACEBOOK: OPTIMIZING FOR CONVERSION

Among the most effective venues for performance marketing is Facebook because of its enormous user base and sophisticated targeting. On Facebook, success goes beyond reach to include increasing conversions. Whether it is a lead, a purchase, or a sign-up, you must maximize your efforts for particular activities to accomplish this.

Example: Airbnb has built a community and gotten more bookings through Facebook by using user-generated content. As part of their "We Are Here" campaign, real stories were shared in video ads with hosts and visitors. By focusing on potential guests who had already shown interest in travel-related content, they saw a big rise in bookings.

Key Tactics:

- **Conversion-Optimized Campaigns:** Use Facebook's conversion optimization tools, like the Conversions API and Pixel, to track user behavior and tailor your ads to people who are most likely to complete the desired action.
- **Dynamic Retargeting:** Facebook's dynamic ads can automatically show products or services that users have previously viewed. This is a powerful way to re-engage users who didn't convert on their first visit and pull them back into the funnel.

Performance Best Practices:

- Keep your creative and messaging simple and action-oriented. Make sure your CTA (Call-to-Action) is clear, like "Sign Up" or "Book Now."
- Run A/B tests on different creatives and audiences to see which combinations drive the highest conversion rates.

- Use Facebook's Lookalike Audiences to find people who are similar to your best customers and expand your reach to a highly relevant audience.

2. INSTAGRAM: DRIVING SALES WITH VISUAL APPEAL

Instagram is the place for visually-driven brands, and its younger audience makes it perfect for D2C businesses aiming to drive immediate actions like sales, lead generation, or app installs. In 2024 Meta's approach for using AI for enhanced experience is a boon for performance marketers. Also, its ad formats allow you to create visually engaging campaigns that push users straight to checkout or sign-up.

Example: Glossier leveraged Instagram's visual-first approach to build a massive following and drive sales. Their strategy revolved around UGC content, encouraging customers to share photos using #Glossier hashtags. These posts not only built trust but also created a ripple effect that directly translated into more sales.

Key Tactics:

- **Part of META:** The best thing for Instagram is it's a part of Meta, i.e., Facebook, which helps not only test the same ad on both platforms simultaneously but also its AI getting advanced every passing day, which you can see in the enhancement feature while setting up the ad.
- **Stories for Quick Conversions:** Use Instagram Stories to offer limited-time promotions or drive users to a landing page with swipe-up functionality. Stories create a sense of urgency and often result in higher conversion rates.

Performance Best Practices:

- Maintain consistency in your visual branding to build trust and recognition.

- Focus on short, impactful videos and carousels to capture attention quickly.
- Retarget users who engage with your posts but haven't made a purchase yet with dynamic ads or personalized offers.

3. TIKTOK: TURN TRENDS INTO CONVERSIONS (NOT FOR INDIA)

TikTok's rapid growth makes it a prize for performance marketing, especially if Gen Z and younger Millennials are in your target audience. This site is all about short, creative, and fun videos, but what makes it really useful for performance marketing is that it can quickly make content go popular. It's not enough to just get views; you need to turn those views into sales.

Example: Chipotle's #GuacDance challenge is a great example of using TikTok for performance marketing. The campaign encouraged users to post fun, dancing videos for a chance to win free guacamole. It went viral and resulted in Chipotle's highest digital sales day ever.

Key Tactics:

- **Leverage TikTok Trends:** To drive results, don't just create ads—tap into trends. Look for viral challenges or popular sounds, and create content that aligns with what's already working on the platform.
- **Influencer Partnerships:** Partner with TikTok influencers who can create authentic content around your product. Influencers often have built-in audiences that trust their recommendations, which can lead to fast conversions.

Performance Best Practices:

- Create short, funny, and real videos. Users of TikTok can tell right away when an ad is overproduced, so focus on being real.
- With TikTok's "Shop Now" button, viewers can easily go from a video to your checkout page.
- Iterate quickly and measure interest. Like TikTok, your efforts should move quickly.

4. LINKEDIN: B2B LEAD GENERATION POWERHOUSE

LinkedIn is where you need to be for B2B performance marketing. Whether you're driving downloads for a whitepaper, gathering leads, or booking demo calls, LinkedIn is built for reaching decision-makers in a professional setting.

Example: HubSpot gets good leads for its sales and marketing tools by using LinkedIn. They are able to contact professionals in the right fields and get them to sign up for webinars, download reports, or ask for demos by using both Sponsored Content and InMail campaigns.

Key Tactics:

- **Sponsored Content with Clear CTAs:** Use LinkedIn's Sponsored Content ads to promote white papers, eBooks, or case studies. Make sure your CTA clearly indicates the next step, whether it's downloading a report or signing up for a demo.
- **Account-Based Marketing (ABM):** LinkedIn's targeting capabilities allow you to focus on specific companies, industries, or job titles. This makes it ideal for ABM campaigns that aim to engage high-value prospects.

Performance Best Practices:

- Keep your content professional but engaging. People on LinkedIn are busy, so make it clear what they'll gain from taking the desired action.
- Use lead-gen forms within LinkedIn ads to reduce friction. These pre-filled forms make it easier for users to convert without leaving the platform.
- Track conversion metrics like cost per lead (CPL) and lead quality to continuously optimize your campaigns.

5. YOUTUBE: LONG-FORM VIDEO WITH HIGH CONVERSION POTENTIAL

YouTube offers an incredible opportunity for performance marketing, especially for brands that have more to say or show about their product. It's a platform for storytelling, but that doesn't mean it's only for branding—YouTube ads can drive serious conversions when done right.

Example: Apple's "Shot on iPhone" effort highlighted actual UGC material on YouTube. The campaign aimed to show the excellence of the iPhone camera, therefore influencing direct sales from people motivated by the material rather than only attitudes.

Key Tactics:

- **TrueView Ads:** Use YouTube's TrueView ads to target specific audiences based on their browsing and search behaviors. Since users can skip these ads, you only pay when they show genuine interest and engage with your content.
- **How-To Videos for Lead Gen:** Create educational or how-to videos that offer value while gently guiding users toward a product or service. Include clear CTAs in the video or description, driving users to your landing page.

Performance Best Practices:

- Make your ad's hook strong. Capture attention within the first five seconds before users can skip.
- Include a strong CTA either visually on the screen or in the video description.
- Use YouTube retargeting to reach users who've interacted with your videos but haven't yet converted.

CONCLUSION: MASTERING PLATFORM-SPECIFIC PERFORMANCE STRATEGIES

Performance marketing is all about having a message and knowing where to put it. You can interact with your followers and get them to do different things on each platform. For example, on Instagram, you can get people to buy something right away, while on LinkedIn, they can sign up for a webinar.

Your success depends on how well you can adapt to the differences between each platform, how well you can optimize for conversions, and how often you test and improve your tactics. If you pick the right platforms and strategies, you can make sure that your efforts have the most impact possible and that you always meet your KPIs.

Chapter 7

Crafting Irresistible CTAs

"Without a sense of urgency, desire loses its value."

– Jim Rohn

INTRODUCTION TO CALLS TO ACTION (CTAS)

The Call to Action (CTA) is the "magic button" of performance marketing. People who were interested but didn't do anything can then get an app, sign up for a service, or buy something. The call to action (CTA) is what makes the sale, not the ad itself.

A good CTA does more than just tell people what to do. You need to know a lot about human behavior, design principles, and how to keep making things better in order to make the right prompt that turns interest into sales. Getting people to do something must be simple, clear, and hard to refuse. This chapter will show you how to make CTAs work even better by breaking down the parts that get a lot of hits.

PSYCHOLOGICAL TRIGGERS FOR EFFECTIVE CTAS

To drive conversions, you need to understand what motivates people to take action. The most effective CTAs tap into human psychology, using carefully chosen words and principles that compel users to act. Here's what you need to consider:

1. Urgency and Scarcity

Creating a sense of urgency or scarcity can dramatically increase the effectiveness of a CTA. Phrases like *"Limited Time Offer," "Ends Tonight,"* or *"Only a Few Left"* tap into our fear of missing out (FOMO), pushing users to act before it's too late. This plays on the psychological desire to avoid loss, which is a powerful motivator.

Example: An e-commerce site might use the CTA, *"Only 3 Left in Stock—Order Now!"* to encourage fast action.

2. Clarity and Specificity

Ambiguity is the enemy of action. A clear and direct CTA tells users exactly what will happen when they click. The more specific you are, the easier it is for users to follow through. Phrases like *"Download*

Your Free Guide" or "*Start Your 14-Day Trial*" leave no room for confusion.

Example: A software company might use the CTA "*Start Your Free 30-Day Trial Now*" to clearly communicate what the user gets and what action they should take.

3. Highlight the Value

People won't do something unless they can see a clear reason to. How does it benefit the person who clicks on your call to action? Whether the benefit is saving money, getting special access, or unlocking a feature, telling people about it right away makes them more likely to take action.

Example: A streaming service might use the CTA "*Watch Ad-Free for $5/Month*" to entice users with a clear value proposition.

4. Personalization

If someone feels like the message is just for them, they are more likely to react. It makes your CTA feel more meaningful if you address the user by name or talk about what they've done before. Personalization can boost engagement significantly because it makes users feel valued.

Example: An online store could use the CTA "*Welcome Back, Sarah! Shop New Arrivals Just for You*" to add a personal touch and make the user feel special.

5. Action-Oriented Language

CTAs work best when they use strong, action-oriented verbs that inspire immediate movement. Words like "*Discover*," "*Get*," "*Join*," "*Claim*," and "*Start*" prompt users to act right now. Avoid passive language, as it lacks urgency and motivation.

Example: A fitness app might use the CTA "*Start Your Free Workout Plan Today*" to create excitement and encourage immediate engagement.

DESIGN PRINCIPLES FOR EFFECTIVE CTAS

Typography and style are just as important as the words in your call to action (CTA). Get people to take action by making CTAs that do the following:

1. Visual Contrast

Your CTA should stand out from the rest of the content. Use contrasting colors and bold fonts to draw attention to it. A CTA that blends in will get overlooked, no matter how compelling the wording. Make sure it's visually distinct from the surrounding elements on the page.

Example: A brightly colored button, like red or orange, on a more neutral background can attract the eye and increase clicks.

2. Size and Placement

The size of your CTA matters. People might miss it if it's too small, and if it's too big, it might feel pushy or too much. Find the right mix and put it where people will naturally look, like above the fold on landing pages or at the end of blog posts.

Example: A centrally placed CTA button at the end of a landing page summary encourages users to take action as soon as they're sold on the value.

3. Simple, Readable Fonts

You should be able to read the words of your CTA at a glance. Simple, bold styles work well on all screen sizes. Don't use fancy or hard-to-read fonts that might make people pause. People can decide faster if the information is easy to read.

Example: A clean, sans-serif font on a high-contrast button ensures that the CTA is both clear and inviting.

4. Whitespace and Minimalism

A crowded page dilutes the power of your CTA. Leave a lot of room around your call to action (CTA) to make it stand out and give people a clear place to focus. It's easier to see what you want to do when the style is simple.

Example: A minimalist CTA button with plenty of space around it and a short, direct message makes it easy for users to understand what they're supposed to do next.

5. Consistent Branding

Your CTA should feel like a natural extension of your brand. Consistent colors, fonts, and styles help build trust and make users feel like they're engaging with a credible business. But balance this consistency with the need for the CTA to stand out.

Example: A CTA button using your brand's core color palette ties into your overall site design, reinforcing the brand while prompting action.

OPTIMIZING CTAS THROUGH TESTING

To improve your CTAs and get the most out of them, you need to test them all the time. Click-through and conversion rates can go up a lot with even small changes to the language or style.

1. A/B Testing

Split testing, also known as A/B testing, looks at two copies of a CTA to see which one works better. Try out different combinations of words, button sizes, colors, and locations to find the best one. If you think something works, try it.

Example: Compare a CTA with the text *"Sign Up Now"* to one with *"Get Instant Access"* to see which generates more clicks.

2. Tracking Performance Metrics

To find out how well your CTAs are working, look at click-through rates (CTR), conversion rates, and bounce rates. These numbers show you if your call-to-actions are getting people to do what you want them to do and where you can make changes.

Example: Monitor how different versions of a CTA perform over time to understand which one drives more conversions.

3. User Feedback

You can get some of the most useful information by asking your viewers directly. Get feedback from people by using polls or user testing to find out how they see your CTAs and what might be stopping them from clicking.

Example: A short survey after the purchase that asks how clear the CTA was could help make future versions better.

4. Iterative Improvements

You don't just do optimization once. People should always test your changes and tell you what they think about them so they work better. Your CTAs should always be best for your audience, so you should change them over time.

Example: If users say the writing isn't clear, change the CTA to make it clearer and test again.

Examples of High-Converting CTAs

Looking at real-world examples of successful CTAs can provide inspiration for crafting your own high-converting CTAs. Here are a few examples from top brands:

Dropbox – "Sign Up for Free"

The Dropbox call to action is a great example of how to keep things easy to understand. Not too much, but just enough to tell people what to do. The word "Free" is very important here because it takes away any question or trouble and makes the deal look like it has little risk.

Why It Works: The word "free" provides an immediate benefit, and the action ("Sign Up") is clear and specific. There's no ambiguity about what will happen next.

Amazon – "Buy Now with One Click"

The well-known Amazon call to action for its one-click buy feature is all about speed and ease. By focusing on simplicity, the CTA gets people to act quickly with little effort by getting rid of the usual multiple-step checkout process.

Why It Works: The combination of "Buy Now" and "One Click" makes it irresistibly simple. The phrase gives a sense of immediacy, leading to higher impulse purchases.

HubSpot – "Get Started Free"

HubSpot's call to action is like Dropbox's, but it focuses on the action of starting. This CTA not only shows the benefit (it's free), but it also quietly urges the user to act right away by saying "Get Started."

Why It Works: The phrase "Get Started" is action-oriented, and the addition of "Free" reassures users that there's no initial cost. It sets clear expectations without any perceived risks.

Nike – "Just Do It"

In performance-based ads, Nike's famous slogan can also be used as a call to action. The phrase is inspiring and fits nicely with Nike's brand values. It doesn't tell people exactly what to do, but it's meant to get them to act right away.

Why It Works: It's short, memorable, and packed with emotional resonance. The urgency and boldness of the message align with Nike's core brand identity.

Spotify – "Try Premium Free"

With the offer of a free trial, Spotify's call to action (CTA) asks users to try out its paid service. This method lowers the entry barrier, letting the user try out premium features without having to make a pledge right away.

Why It Works: The word "Try" suggests that it's easy and risk-free, while "Premium" highlights the exclusivity and value. Together, they push users toward an immediate decision.

Advanced Techniques for Crafting High-Impact CTAs

To further boost the effectiveness of your CTAs, you can incorporate more advanced strategies to maximize conversion potential:

1. Dynamic CTAs

A dynamic CTA changes depending on who the user is or where they are in the customer journey. By personalizing CTAs based on user data (like location, purchase history, or behavior), you can make them far more relevant and engaging.

Example: A returning user might see a CTA that says, "*Welcome Back! Shop Your Favorites,*" while a new user sees, "*Join and Get 10% Off Your First Purchase.*"

2. Interactive CTAs

Interactive CTAs invite users to engage more actively, creating a more personalized experience. For example, you could use a quiz or slider that leads users toward a product or service based on their preferences.

Example: A clothing retailer might use an interactive CTA that asks, "*Find Your Perfect Fit,*" which leads users through a short quiz to recommend products based on their style.

3. Social Proof Integration

Adding social proof to your call to action (CTA) can increase sales and build trust by showing people that other people have already taken action. "Join 100,000+ Happy Customers" or "Over 5 Million Users and Counting" messages comfort users and make them want to keep going.

Example: A software company might use a CTA like *"Join 50,000 Businesses Using Our Platform"* to create credibility and reduce hesitation.

4. Exit-Intent Popups

Felt like exiting the landing page, website, or app? If a website user is about to leave, a call to action (CTA) will be shown. You can get a lot of last-minute sales by letting people know about a deal or the store right before they leave.

Example: An e-commerce site might use an exit-intent CTA like *"Wait! Get 15% Off Before You Go"* to convert abandoning visitors into buyers.

Conclusion: Mastering the Craft of High-Converting CTAs

Making a compelling CTA is both an art and a science. It requires understanding how people think and feel, using design ideas well, and constantly improving performance. The best CTAs are those that are tailored to the wants and goals of the users. This way, they naturally lead them to take action instead of just telling them what to do.

You can turn a simple prompt into a powerful tool that boosts sales by using clear, interesting language, good design, and smart placement. Whether you're selling a product, capturing leads, or growing your subscriber base, mastering the CTA can dramatically improve your campaign outcomes.

Remember, every interaction your audience has with your CTA is an opportunity to drive meaningful action. Use the principles and techniques in this chapter to create CTAs that not only capture attention but convert that attention into real, measurable results for your business.

Chapter 8

Data-Driven Creativity

"Information is the oil of the 21st century, and analytics is the combustion engine."

– Peter Sondergaard

INTRODUCTION TO DATA-DRIVEN CREATIVITY

Marketers can't just guess or go with their gut when it comes to making ads that work in today's fast-paced digital world. In performance marketing, where the goal is not just to get people's attention but also to get results that can be measured, it's important to combine data with imagination. Data can help marketer make ads that work, but they still need to be creative. Ads that really work and have a bigger effect can be made when artistic ideas are mixed with data insights.

This chapter talks about how to find the right mix between facts and creativity so that you can come up with new advertising ideas that sell a lot of stuff.

THE ROLE OF CREATIVITY IN PERFORMANCE MARKETING

Making ads stand out comes down to being creative. It's what draws people in, makes them feel things, and gives them stories they'll remember. But in performance marketing, being creative isn't enough on its own. It needs to be clear, current, and most importantly, able to get people to act. This is where the facts come in.

If you have creative ideas, you can use data to make sure they reach the right people at the right time. It can let you know if your message is getting through or not, and it can give you ideas that can help you improve and refine your artistic approach. The best ads, on the other hand, use data to boost creativity, not take it away..

Example: Apple's "Think Different" campaign is often hailed as a creative triumph, but what made it especially powerful was how well it tapped into what Apple's audience valued—innovation and individuality. While the campaign was beautifully creative, it was also grounded in consumer insights that allowed Apple to speak directly to their customers' aspirations.

THE INTERSECTION OF DATA AND CREATIVITY

A lot of the time, people think that facts and imagination are opposites, but they work really well together. The data points you in the right direction, but the story comes to life in your mind. How do they work together?

1. **Data-Informed Creativity:** Data gives you insights into what your audience responds to—what they engage with, what they ignore, and what drives them to take action. This allows your creative team to craft ads that not only look good but also resonate deeply with your audience.

Example: A brand might find that funny content really connects with their audience by looking at engagement data on social media. This information can then be used to make sure that humor is used in future campaigns so that they get more people to connect and buy.

2. **Creative Testing and Optimization:** Data isn't just helpful for making plans; it's also necessary for improving artistic work. You can A/B test different forms of your ad with performance marketing to find the best one. You can fine-tune your campaigns for best impact by using data to see which parts—whether it's the headline, the images, or the tone—are getting results.

Example: An online store might have two different ads for the same product. One would show the product being used, and the other would show the product in a more ideal living setting. The store can see which creative method gets better results and make changes based on that by comparing click-through rates and conversions.

3. **Real-Time Analytics for Immediate Adjustments:** One of the best things about digital ads is that you can see how it's doing right now. This means you can change how you're being creative at any time based on how it's going. You don't have to wait until the campaign is over to fix your ad if it's not working. You can change the idea in the middle of the campaign to get better results.

Example: Let's say you're running a campaign for display ads, and early data shows that one version of your ad isn't doing very well. With real-time analytics, you can see which parts aren't working—maybe it's the picture or the call to action—and make quick changes to make it work better.

BALANCING DATA AND CREATIVITY

While data is essential, too much of it can stifle creativity. The key is finding a balance between the two—letting data inform your creative decisions without letting it dictate every move. Here's how to strike that balance:

1. **Avoid Data Overload:** It's easy to fall into the trap of overanalyzing data, which can lead to decision paralysis. While it's important to use data as a guide, creativity requires freedom and flexibility. Don't let data turn your campaign into a formula—there's always room for a creative spark.

Example: Maybe your data shows that blue buttons convert better than red ones, but that doesn't mean every creative decision should be dictated by this one insight. Instead, let creativity lead while keeping data in mind.

2. **Foster a Creative-First Culture:** Even in a data-driven workplace, your team should feel free to try new things and take risks. Get people to come up with ideas and explore

their creativity, and use data to improve those ideas instead of limiting them.

Example: Even in a data-driven workplace, your team should feel free to try new things and take risks. Get people to come up with ideas and explore their creativity, and use data to improve those ideas instead of limiting them.

3. **Integrate Data into the Creative Process:** Rather than viewing data as something that happens after the fact, bring it into the creative process from the start. Use data to uncover trends and opportunities that can inspire your creative direction.

Example: If search data shows a growing interest in eco-friendly products, this could inspire a creative campaign that taps into this trend by highlighting your brand's commitment to sustainability.

TECHNIQUES FOR DATA-DRIVEN CREATIVE DECISIONS

If you want your campaigns to have the most impact possible, you need to use data in all of your creative choices. How to do it:

1. **Audience Segmentation:** Use data to segment your audience based on behaviors, interests, and demographics. This allows you to tailor your creative for each segment, ensuring your message is relevant and personalized.

Example: A fashion brand might make an ad for young employees that focuses on trendy styles that are good for the office and another ad for retirees that focuses on comfortable clothes for fun.

2. **Content Personalization:** Your content will perform better the more tailored it is. Using user data—such as surfing behavior or purchase patterns—you may create tailored content that seems relevant to every one of the individual users.

Example: An e-commerce site might use personalized CTAs like, *"Complete Your Collection with This Recommended Item,"* based on the user's past shopping habits.

3. **Predictive Analytics:** Predictive analytics allows you to stay ahead of the curve by estimating future trends and behaviors. Using analytics to forecast what your audience will care about next allows you to create innovative campaigns that fulfill their needs before they are aware of them.

Example: Analytical modeling could show that people are interested in items that are good for their health. You could start a campaign to get people to buy your brand's healthy and organic products right before the trend hits its peak.

4. **Competitive Analysis:** You don't always need to start from scratch. By looking at the creative strategies and results of your rivals, you can learn what works in your industry and where you can set yourself apart.

Example: By studying a competitor's successful ad campaign, you might notice they've effectively used user-generated content to build trust. You could adapt this tactic to your brand, finding a way to make it unique to your own audience.

CASE STUDIES OF DATA-DRIVEN CREATIVITY

You can see how data-driven inspiration works in the real world. Here are some examples of how powerful it can be to use both data and creative plan together:

- **Coca-Cola's "Share a Coke" Campaign**: Coca-Cola looked at data to see what words and sentences people liked, and then they used those in their ads. Customers love this kind of personalization, which led to a big rise in interaction and sales.

- **Spotify's "Wrapped" Campaign**: The year-in-review promotion on Spotify uses user data to make personalized playlists and insights that people then share on social media. Spotify's most interesting yearly promotion is the one that uses both data and creative storytelling. .
- **Airbnb's "Live There" Campaign**: Airbnb used information about how people like to travel to make an ad that promoted unique experiences in the area. This method based on data made the campaign very relevant and interesting to travelers who want to experience real things.

CONCLUSION: THE SYNERGY OF DATA AND CREATIVITY

You don't have to guess what will work anymore. Today, data and new ideas go hand in hand in performance marketing. Not only can you make ads that get people's attention, but you can also make ads that get real, measured results.

There are many choices when math and creativity are used together. You're not just making ads; you're also making experiences that connect with people and help you do better. To take your marketing to a whole new level, use how facts and creativity can work together.

Chapter 9

Ethics and Authenticity in Performance Marketing

"Play fair, be prepared for others to play dirty, and don't let them drag you into the mud."

– Richard Branson

A STARTER GUIDE TO ETHICS AND AUTHENTICITY

This day and age, ads and messages are all the time, so brands need more than just a great product to do well. People want to trust the company they buy from. This is where morals and being honest come in. Return on ad spend (ROAS), sales, and clicks are the building blocks of performance marketing. It's not only the right thing to do to be honest and follow the rules, but it's also good business. Sincerity and ethics are very important in performance marketing. This chapter talks about why and how brands can use them to make things last longer, work better, and build trust.

THE TWO-EDGED SWORD OF CONSUMER SKEPTICISM

People are less trusting than ever before. They have so much information at their fingertips that it's easy for them to spot a false claim or an unfair campaign. Now you know why honesty and openness aren't just choices for performance marketers—they're needs. It might work for a while if you trick or lie to people, but it will catch up with you

- **Informed Shoppers**: It only takes a few steps for people to check the facts of what you say. There's no longer any lying when it comes to a product's price, quality, or customer service. It's more important than ever to be honest about what you're selling.

  Example: *Glow Naturals*, a small skin care brand, uses honest advertising by clearly stating in their performance ads what ingredients are in their goods and how they can help your skin. Instead of making broad claims like "natural glow," they focus on how particular ingredients like vitamin C and aloe vera work, which builds trust and leads to more sales.

- **The Impact of Social Media**: Social platforms can spread a negative review just as fast as a positive one. A misleading ad can trigger a backlash that damages your brand's credibility overnight. **Example**: When *Bean Box*, a small coffee subscription service, received criticism on social media for not being transparent about delivery times, they quickly addressed the issue by updating their website with clear shipping details. They also started sending customers real-time updates on their orders. This action not only helped them regain trust but also increased repeat subscriptions.

TRANSPARENCY: THE TRUST BUILDER

A lot of the time, confidence is what makes performance marketing work. Being open and honest can help you get more sales, keep more customers, and make them more loyal to your brand.

- **Clear Communication**: People like messages that are clear and honest. It's important to be clear about things like prices, product information, and how your business works. Performance marketers should stay away from making unclear claims or using small print that isn't clear because it can lead to customers being let down. **Example**: *Happy Paws*, a small business that sells pet supplies, advertised their eco-friendly dog toys on Facebook. They didn't just say that their products were "eco-friendly"; they also explained how they made them in a way that was good for the earth, listing the benefits of each material. More people clicked through and bought things because the message was clear
- **Open Business Practices**: It's more open when people talk about where their goods come from, how they're

made, or even how they're priced. Customers like it when businesses are honest and open because they let them know what's going on behind the scenes. **Example**: *The Ethical Wardrobe*, an online store that sells eco-friendly clothes, uses Google Ads that lead to product pages with a "Cost Transparency" part. This part breaks down how much the materials, work, and markups cost. Customers love how honest it is, which leads to more sales and longer-term customer trust.

ETHICAL PERSUASION VS. MANIPULATION

The goal of performance marketing is to get someone to buy your goods or service. But sometimes it's hard to tell the difference between convincing someone and tricking them. Persuasion honors the customer's right to make an informed choice, but manipulation twists the truth to get someone to buy something. Giving people the information they need to make smart choices is at the heart of ethical performance marketing.

- **Ethical Persuasion**: Clearly and honestly outlining the benefits of your product is essential. To persuade ethically, use verified statements, transparent product specifications, and authentic customer reviews.

  Example: *GreenLeaf Supplements* uses real customer reviews and scientific evidence to show how their goods can help people in their Facebook ads. They also promise to give you your money back. This honest and moral method helps customers trust you and consistently leads to sales.

- **Avoiding Manipulative Tactics**: Trying to get people to buy by using scary messages or false claims can fail. For a short time, manipulation might work, but in the long run, it usually ends with unhappy customers, a lot of returns, and a bad image.

Example: A small fitness brand, *FitFuel Nutrition*, avoided manipulative tactics by not using "limited time only" pressure in their Google Ads. Instead, they focused on promoting free samples and offering genuine value. This approach boosted trust, decreased cart abandonment, and led to better overall conversion rates.

BUILDING AN AUTHENTIC BRAND IDENTITY

Authenticity isn't just a buzzword. It's a foundation for building real, meaningful connections with your audience. In performance marketing, where every ad dollar counts, a strong and authentic brand identity can lead to better engagement, stronger conversion rates, and higher customer lifetime value.

- **Consistency is Key**: Brands that are consistent in their messaging and actions are more likely to be trusted. If your marketing says one thing, but your product delivers another, customers will notice.

  Example: *Loom & Thread* is a small business that makes textiles by hand. They are committed to ecology and quality. Their Instagram ads show the real artists who make each item and the time-consuming steps they take to make their homemade goods. Higher interest and conversion rates came from the fact that their brand story and ads were consistent.

- **Genuine Engagement**: Being honest with your audience by responding to comments or handling concerns in an open way builds relationships that last and makes your marketing work better.

Example: *Sipsy*, a boutique tea company, builds authenticity by engaging with customers on social media, often replying personally to comments and DMs. They also run performance ads offering personalized tea recommendations based on user preferences. This genuine connection helped them increase their repeat customer rate and improve ad performance.

SOCIAL CAUSES AND CORPORATE RESPONSIBILITY

Brands that authentically support social causes and align with corporate responsibility can create strong, meaningful connections with their audience. However, it's crucial to do it genuinely and not simply as a marketing tactic.

- **Meaningful Support**: If you're aligning your brand with a social cause, make sure it's a real commitment and not just lip service. Consumers can spot when a brand is being inauthentic.

  Example: *Pure Roots*, a small organic skincare brand, donates a portion of its profits to environmental cleanup efforts. Their performance marketing campaigns on Google Ads highlight their real contributions to these causes, showing measurable results rather than just a feel-good message. This genuine connection with their cause helped improve their conversion rates and customer loyalty.

- **Avoiding "Woke-Washing"**: Simply jumping on a social cause for the sake of appearing trendy can backfire. Make sure your brand's actions reflect the social values you're promoting.

  Example: *Haven Yoga Studio* had a successful YouTube ad campaign that showed how they helped underserved communities by giving people who couldn't pay for lessons free ones. People really liked how committed they were to being welcoming, which led to more people signing up and a good impression of the brand.

BEST PRACTICES FOR ETHICAL PERFORMANCE MARKETING

1. **Commit to Transparency**: Be upfront about your product features, pricing, and business practices. Honest communication helps consumers trust your brand and drives better performance.
2. **Engage Authentically**: Respond to customer concerns and feedback in a genuine way. Personalized engagement leads to better conversion rates and long-term loyalty.
3. **Align Actions with Values**: Make sure your brand's marketing and practices reflect your stated values. Customers appreciate brands that practice what they preach.
4. **Adapt and Improve**: Monitor customer feedback and performance metrics to continually optimize your marketing strategies while staying true to your values.
5. **Educate Your Team:** Make sure that everyone on your marketing team knows how important ethical advertising is and how to include it in campaigns.

CONCLUSION: WHY ETHICS AND HONESTY ARE IMPORTANT

Being honest and moral can help you stand out from other marketers in performance marketing, which is based on views, results, and sales. Trust and long-term success can come to brands that are honest, don't try to trick people, and stay true to their core values. Remember that ethical marketing is more than just a plan. In a world with a lot of competition, it's the only way to make connections that last and grow your business.

Chapter 10

Future-Proofing Your Advertising Strategies for Performance Marketing

"The future belongs to those who learn more skills and combine them in creative ways."

– Robert Greene

HOW TO GET AHEAD IN A WORLD THAT CHANGES ALL THE TIME.

New technologies and changes in how people act are making the business world change quickly. It's tough for small companies that use performance marketing to stay on top of these changes and figure out how to use them to grow in a way that can be tracked. In this chapter, we'll talk about some important trends, such as personalized AI, virtual reality (AR), and sustainability. We'll also talk about some other ways to make your performance marketing efforts more stable for the future, which will lead to higher ad spend returns, sales, and customer retention.

WHAT'S NEW IN PERFORMANCE MARKETING?

AI-based personalization

Small businesses can now use AI to make their ads more relevant to users by learning about their likes and dislikes. This is changing the future of advertising. With the help of tools like machine learning algorithms and dynamic creative optimization, brands can make ads that are very specific to people and get more interaction and sales.

Machine Learning for Predictive Targeting:: AI can help small businesses look at old data and guess how customers will act in the future, which will help them do a better job of marketing. This makes sure that ads get to the right people at the right time without having to guess.

Example: A small brand, *EcoPet Treats,* makes natural pet food. They used machine learning algorithms to make Facebook ads that are more relevant to people who buy a lot of pet products. Their 30% increase in ad clicks led to a 20% rise in sales over six months.

CHATBOTS FOR LEAD NURTURING AND CONVERSIONS

You need apps that are controlled by AI if you want to turn visitors into leads and customers. The sales process can be moved by chatbots without any help from a person. This is because they can engage customers right away and answer their questions.

Example: *GreenHaven Garden Tools*, a small online store, set up a robot that could take orders, answer questions about products, and offer tools based on what the customer would like. Sales went up by 15% because the bot was available 24 hours a day, seven days a week to help buyers.

Augmented Reality (AR) for Enhanced Shopping Experiences

AR is a cool tool for small businesses, especially those that sell things like clothes, home decor, or beauty products that look better in person. AR makes shopping more enjoyable and gives people the courage to buy, which results in more sales.

Example: A small store called *Luxe Frames* added augmented reality (AR) to their website so that people could try on different frames visually. People were more interested, which made them feel better about their choices, which led to 18% more online sales.

Sustainability as a Performance Driver

People today, particularly Gen Z and Millennials, care a lot about the environment and doing the right thing. Not only is supporting an environment good for your brand, it also helps your business do well. Adding sustainability to the performance marketing plans of small businesses can help them get more customers and keep the ones they already have.

Example: The small company *EarthFresh* packing, which sells biodegradable food containers, used the phrases "zero-waste" and "sustainable packaging" in its Google Ads. People who care about the environment were the ones who bought more, which led to a

35% rise in sales. Many customers said that sustainability was the reason they bought.

ADAPTING TO CONSUMER BEHAVIOR IN PERFORMANCE MARKETING

Leveraging Micro-Influencers for Performance

Today, small companies can benefit from working with micro-influencers, who are social media stars with small but active followings. This is because influencer marketing has changed over the years. It's often more cost-effective to work with small influencers than with big ones for performance marketing, and the effects can be seen right away, like sales, sign-ups, or downloads.

Example: *Vitality Herbals* is a small business that makes natural supplements. They worked with a group of "micro-influencers" who are into fitness to promote their products on Instagram through stories and posts. There was a 10X return on ad spend (ROAS) because more people bought things on the website.

Subscription Models and Recurring Revenue

Most small businesses these days get a lot of their revenue from service plans. If a business lets customers subscribe to things or services, they can make more money and get a higher customer lifetime value (CLV). When it comes to performance marketing, this means focusing on ways to keep customers instead of getting new ones all the time, since keeping customers can be cheaper.

Example: The food kit delivery service FreshFlavors used retargeting ads to get in touch with people who had bought from them before but hadn't bought anything else. The cost of getting a new customer (CAC) went down and they got 20% more users by giving deals to people who signed up for a subscription plan.

HARNESSING DATA AND ANALYTICS FOR PERFORMANCE MARKETING

Using Customer Data to Drive Decisions

A lot of information is used in performance marketing, which helps small businesses figure out what works and what doesn't. Google Ads, Facebook, and email marketing can all do better if you use customer data for A/B testing, segmenting, and advertising.

Example: *Savvy Prints*, a small print-on-demand business, used Google Analytics to track their customers' actions and discovered that people who read product reviews were 40% more likely to buy something. When those people were shown Google Display ads with customer reviews again, the number of conversions went up by 25%.

Attribution Models for Better ROI Tracking

It can be hard for small businesses to figure out which links lead to sales. There are models that can help you keep track of and improve all of your interactions with a customer, from the first click to the last purchase. You can be sure that your marketing money is well spent this way.

Example: This is how *Urban Gear Co.*, an outdoor gear company, moved from last-click attribution to a multi-touch model that showed them the value of things like video ads and social media interactions that happen earlier in the sales funnel. Their work got better as a result, which led to 15% more sales and 10% lower acquisition costs.

EMBRACING NEW TECHNOLOGIES FOR PERFORMANCE MARKETING

Voice Search Optimization

As more people get smart systems like Alexa and Google Home, voice search is growing in popularity. When it comes to local searches, voice search optimization can help small businesses get more people and make more sales.

Example: For *Baked Bliss*, a small bakery, voice search queries like "best bakery near me" and "order cupcakes for delivery" were made to work best. In just three months, call searches brought in 12% more business in their area.

Programmatic Advertising for Smarter Campaigns

Programmatic advertising uses algorithms and big data to show ads to specific people at the right time and place. It can help save money by reducing waste and using resources more efficiently. This is what will help you get the most out of your money (ROI).

Example: A little furniture business called *Rustic Homes Furniture* used automated ads to reach people who had been to home decor websites not long ago. This made their ads work better overall and cut their cost per acquisition (CPA) by 40%.

LONG-TERM STRATEGIES FOR SUSTAINABLE PERFORMANCE MARKETING

Making a marketing team that can change as needed

A small business must be able to act quickly. For performance marketing to work in the long term, you need to be able to quickly change direction and adjust to new platforms, trends, and customer habits. This means pushing people to "test and learn," which means that they can quickly look at small experiments and do bigger ones if they work.

Example: A small flower delivery service called *PetalPerks* quickly tests two different versions of their Facebook ads to see which one gets the most hits. They quickly found the ads that worked best and ran more of them. This helped them double their conversion rates while keeping costs low.

Investing in Lifetime Customer Value

Going after new people isn't always the best way to grow. Sometimes, the growth is too fast to keep up. It's better for small businesses to keep people and figure out how much they're worth over time (LTV). People will buy from you again and again if you use personalized email marketing, loyalty programs, and ways to keep people excited after they've bought something.

Example: A small store called *BrightBox* Lighting sells LED lights. As a prize for customers' loyalty, the store created a loyalty program that lets them save money on future purchases. 30% more repeat sales and 25% more worth over the life of a customer were made possible by this project.

CONCLUSION: FUTURE-PROOFING YOUR PERFORMANCE MARKETING STRATEGY

Small businesses must always be changing in order to keep up with how performance marketing is changing. You can stay alive and even do well if you use AI, AR, voice search, care about the environment, and make decisions based on facts. Keep customers, use attribution models, and give each person a unique experience to get the best return on investment (ROI). Make sure that the things you do have long-lasting effects that you can measure.

To make your advertising plans work in the future, you will need to be flexible, pay attention to data, and put the customer first. This is because people's tastes change quickly. Your business will do well in performance marketing if you are open to new ideas and committed to giving value. This is true whether you are trying out new tools or making methods that have already worked better.

Bonus Chapter

Creating Ads That Truly Convert

"The best marketing doesn't feel like marketing."

– Tom Fishburne

INTRODUCTION: THE GAME CHANGER IN ADVERTISING

Advertising used to be mostly about grabbing people's attention. In the digital sphere, now, it's all about motivating people to act. Showing you how to transform views into clicks, clicks into conversions, and conversions into devoted consumers, this additional chapter delves into great depth on the elements that make ads successful. You will learn how to create advertising that produce results, come up with viral hooks that cause people to pause and consider, and craft tales directly for your audience.

1. VIRAL HOOKS: CAPTURING ATTENTION IN SECONDS

In the crowded world of digital advertising, your content needs to stand out immediately. A viral hook is a powerful tool that grabs attention and makes your ad memorable. Here's how to create hooks that resonate:

- **Understanding the Hook**: A hook is a captivating element in your ad that draws viewers in from the start. This could be an unexpected image, a bold statement, a shocking statistic, or a compelling question. Hooks should trigger curiosity, surprise, or emotion, prompting viewers to continue engaging with your content.
- **Types of Viral Hooks**:
    - **Visual Hooks**: Use striking or unusual visuals to make an immediate impact. Think of a celebrity appearance, a unique setting, or eye-catching graphics. Visual hooks work well in platforms like Instagram and TikTok, where users are scrolling quickly.
    - **Emotional Hooks**: Tapping into core emotions—like happiness, anger, fear, or love—can create a strong

connection with your audience. Ads that evoke emotions are more likely to be shared, which can increase virality.

  - **Curiosity Hooks**: Create an element of mystery that makes viewers want to learn more. Use questions, teasers, or cliffhangers to build intrigue. Phrases like "You won't believe what happens next..." or "The secret to..." are classic examples.
  - **Storytelling Hooks**: Begin with an engaging story that audiences can relate to. Stories draw people in by creating empathy and relatability. Use real-life scenarios, customer testimonials, or a narrative arc to engage viewers emotionally.

- **Crafting Your Viral Hook**:
  - Start with a bold statement or question.
  - Use vivid, compelling imagery.
  - Create a sense of urgency, or FOMO (Fear of Missing Out).
  - Use humor, surprise, or shock value to grab attention.

2. WRITING HIGH-CONVERTING SCRIPTS: THE ART OF PERSUASION

A well-crafted script is the backbone of any successful ad campaign. It's the narrative that guides your audience from curiosity to action. Here's how to write scripts that convert:

- **Know Your Audience**: The first step in writing a high-converting script is understanding who you're speaking to. Identify your target audience's pain points, needs, and desires. Use language that resonates with them—speak their language, understand their challenges, and show empathy.

- **The Structure of a High-Converting Script**:
    - **Opening Hook**: Start with a hook that grabs attention immediately—whether it's a bold statement, a powerful visual, or an emotional appeal.
    - **Problem Statement**: Clearly define the problem your product or service solves. Make it relatable and urgent; the audience should feel the pain point.
    - **Unique Selling Proposition (USP)**: Highlight what makes your product or service different. This is your moment to shine and differentiate from competitors.
    - **Emotional Appeal**: Connect with your audience on an emotional level. Tell a story or use imagery that makes them feel something—joy, fear, excitement, etc.
    - **Call to Action (CTA)**: End with a strong, clear CTA that tells the audience exactly what to do next—"Buy Now," "Sign Up Today," "Learn More," etc.
- **Techniques for Writing High-Converting Scripts**:
    - **Use Clear, Concise Language**: Avoid jargon or complex phrases. Keep it simple and direct.
    - **Focus on Benefits, Not Features**: Emphasize how the product will improve the customer's life. For example, instead of saying, "Our vacuum has a 2000-watt motor," say, "Our vacuum will clean your home in half the time."
    - **Incorporate Social Proof**: Mention testimonials, reviews, or endorsements from satisfied customers or industry experts.
    - **Use a Conversational Tone**: Write as if you're having a conversation with the viewer. Use "you" and "your" to make it personal and engaging.

- **Leverage Storytelling**: Use anecdotes or personal stories to illustrate the benefits of your product or service.

3. ELEMENTS NEEDED FOR HIGH-CONVERTING ADS

Every successful ad is built on the foundation of key elements that work together to drive conversions. Here are the must-have components:

- **Compelling Visuals**: Humans are visual creatures; we process images much faster than text. Use high-quality, eye-catching visuals that align with your brand and message. Whether it's a stunning photo, a vibrant graphic, or an engaging video, visuals should immediately convey the essence of your ad.
- **Clear and Bold Headline**: The headline is often the first text that people see, so it needs to grab attention and convey the ad's main message. It should be concise, direct, and impactful—aim for no more than 6-8 words.
- **Persuasive Body Copy**: This is where you provide more details about your product or service. Focus on benefits over features and use storytelling techniques to engage the reader. Keep sentences short and avoid complex jargon.
- **Strong Call to Action (CTA)**: A CTA is crucial for converting interest into action. It should be clear, concise, and compelling. Use actionable language like "Buy Now," "Join Today," or "Get Started." Position the CTA strategically within the ad to make it easily noticeable.
- **Social Proof**: People are more likely to trust your product if they see that others have had positive experiences with it. Incorporate reviews, testimonials, or endorsements to build credibility and trust.

- **Value Proposition**: Clearly state what makes your product or service unique. Why should customers choose you over the competition? This could be a unique feature, a special discount, or an added benefit that competitors don't offer.
- **Urgency and Scarcity**: Create a sense of urgency or scarcity to encourage immediate action. Use phrases like "Limited Time Offer," "Only a Few Left," or "Offer Ends Soon" to prompt viewers to act now rather than later.
- **Personalization**: Tailor your ad content to different segments of your audience. Use data to deliver personalized messaging that speaks directly to the consumer's needs, preferences, and behaviors.

4. HIGH-CONVERTING AD COPY: THE BUILDING BLOCKS OF PERSUASION

Great ad copy isn't just about what you say; it's about how you say it. Here's how to write ad copy that drives conversions:

- **Headline**: The headline should immediately grab attention and convey the main benefit of your product or service. Use power words like "Free," "New," "Exclusive," and "Guaranteed" to capture interest.
- **Subheadline**: If your ad allows for it, use a subheadline to provide additional context or reinforce the main message. This can further explain the benefit or address a key pain point.
- **Body Copy**: Focus on benefits, not just features. Instead of saying "Our software has a robust CRM," say "Easily manage all your customer relationships in one place and boost your sales by 30%." Use bullet points to break up text and make it easy to read.

- **Urgency and Scarcity**: Incorporate phrases that create a sense of urgency, such as "Act Now," "Limited Time," or "While Supplies Last." Scarcity can drive immediate action by triggering the fear of missing out.
- **CTA (Call to Action)**: A strong, direct CTA tells your audience exactly what to do next. Use action-oriented language and make the CTA stand out visually.
- **A/B Testing Your Ad Copy**: Always test different versions of your ad copy to see what works best. Change one variable at a time (like the headline or CTA) to identify which elements drive the highest engagement and conversion rates.

5. ADVANCED TECHNIQUES FOR BOOSTING AD PERFORMANCE

- **Retargeting and Remarketing**: Use retargeting strategies to bring back users who have shown interest but haven't converted. Remarketing ads can remind them of the benefits, offer an incentive, or address any objections they may have.
- **Dynamic Ads**: Use dynamic ads that automatically adjust content to show the most relevant products or services to individual users. This personalization increases the likelihood of conversion by catering directly to user interests.
- **Influencer Partnerships**: Collaborate with influencers who align with your brand values and have a strong following in your target market. Influencers can provide authentic endorsements that enhance trust and credibility.
- **User-Generated Content (UGC)**: Encourage customers to create content about your brand. UGC, like reviews,

testimonials, or social media posts, can serve as powerful social proof and drive higher engagement.

- **Interactive Elements**: Incorporate interactive elements like quizzes, polls, or clickable links that engage users and encourage them to spend more time with your ad. Interactive ads are more engaging and can increase conversions by providing a personalized experience.
- **Mobile Optimization**: Ensure your ads are optimized for mobile devices. More than half of all internet traffic comes from mobile devices, so your ads need to be mobile-friendly to reach the widest audience.

6. CRAFTING THE PERFECT AD FUNNEL

An effective ad campaign is about more than just a single ad; it's about the entire funnel—from awareness to conversion. Here's how to build an ad funnel that maximizes conversions:

- **Top of Funnel (TOFU) - Awareness**: At this stage, your goal is to capture attention and build awareness of your brand. Use viral hooks and engaging content to draw people in. Focus on ads that tell a compelling story, highlight the benefits of your product, and create intrigue.
- **Middle of Funnel (MOFU) - Consideration**: Here, your goal is to build trust and encourage consideration. Use retargeting ads to reach people who have engaged with your TOFU content. Provide more in-depth information about your product, such as testimonials, case studies, or detailed features.
- **Bottom of Funnel (BOFU) - Conversion**: The focus here is on closing the sale. Use ads with strong CTAs, limited-time offers, or exclusive discounts to encourage immediate

action. Ensure that your messaging is direct and emphasizes the urgency or scarcity of your offer.

7. TOOLS AND RESOURCES FOR CREATING HIGH-CONVERTING ADS

- **Ad Design Tools**: Tools like Canva, Adobe Spark, and Figma can help you create visually compelling ads without needing advanced design skills.
- **Copywriting Resources**: Use resources like Hemingway Editor or Grammarly to refine your copy and ensure it is clear, concise, and free of errors.
- **Analytics and Testing Tools**: Utilize platforms like Google Analytics, Facebook Ads Manager, or Hotjar to track the performance of your ads and gain insights into user behavior.
- **A/B Testing Platforms**: Tools like Optimizely, VWO, and Unbounce help you run A/B tests on different ad elements to find the highest-performing versions.

8. COMMON PITFALLS TO AVOID IN AD CREATION

- **Overcomplicating Your Message**: Keep it simple. Focus on one key message or benefit.
- **Neglecting Mobile Optimization**: Ensure your ads are mobile-friendly to reach the largest audience possible.
- **Ignoring Audience Segmentation**: Avoid targeting a broad audience. Segment your audience and tailor your ads to specific groups for better relevance.

- **Forgetting to Test and Optimize**: Never launch a campaign without A/B testing. Continuously test and optimize to improve performance.

CONCLUSION: MASTERING THE ART OF HIGH-CONVERTING ADS

It takes both art and science to make ads that get people to buy. It takes a mix of creativity, strategic thinking, and making decisions based on facts. You can make campaigns that not only get people's attention but also get real results if you learn the techniques in this chapter. These include how to write high-converting scripts and viral hooks and how to understand the most important parts of a high-converting ad.

When you advertise online, you have a lot of options. If you know what to do, your ads can be very useful for your business. You can improve your promoting and get the results you want by using the tips in this chapter.

Conclusion & Summary

"Ignoring online marketing is like opening a business and not telling anyone."

– KB Marketing Agency

As we come to the end of this look into the art and science of modern advertising, it's worth thinking about how the different topics we've talked about here fit together to create campaigns that get people to act. Advertising is always changing and complicated because technology is always getting better and people's standards are always changing. But the basic ideas behind good advertising haven't changed over time. They are based on knowing your audience well and being able to connect with them in a useful way.

Chapter 1: Cracking the Consumer Code was the first part of our journey. It helped us understand how current consumers think and feel. Today, we talked about the mental triggers and patterns of behavior that affect choices to buy. Understanding this is important for coming up with tactics that work with today's smart, choice- and information-happy customers.

Chapter 2: Emotional Resonance—The Heart of Effective Ads, In this chapter, we learned more about how to connect with people on an emotional level. We looked into why ads that play on strong feelings like fear, joy, and desire are more likely to get people's attention and build relationships that last. Emotional resonance is more than just getting people's attention; it's about making a deeper, more personal link with them that leads to brand loyalty and affinity.

Chapter 3: The Power of Simplicity - Less Is More, we talked about how important it is to be clear when communicating. In a time when too much knowledge is common, keeping things simple can be very helpful. Ads with clear, concise wording and simple design stand out from the rest, making sure that the main message is both memorable and powerful. This chapter emphasized how keeping your message and design simple can help your brand stand out and make a better impact.

Chapter 4: Building a Brand Identity that Sticks talked about how important it is to have a brand identity that makes sense and is interesting. We talked about how a strong, recognizable brand has a clear set of ideals, a clear voice, and consistent visual elements. In a competitive market, building a strong brand name helps connect with customers and makes it easier for people to recognize your brand.

Chapter 5: Storyselling—Beyond Storytelling looked at how storytelling changed over time to become "storyselling." We learned how to write successful advertising narratives that combine interesting stories with clear sales goals. Being real and relatable is important when writing stories that connect with people and bring in sales. This chapter talked about how important it is to tell stories that are in line with your brand's ideals and get people to care more deeply about your products.

Chapter 6: The Medium is the Message Choosing the Right Channels helped us choose the best advertising sites for our business. We looked at how different outlets, like search engines, social media, and traditional media, offer different chances and need different approaches. The chapter emphasized how important it is to have consistent messaging across all channels in order to have the most effect and reach.

Chapter 7: Crafting Irresistible CTAs talked about how to make calls to action work psychologically. We looked at what makes a call to action (CTA) interesting and how to use A/B testing and other techniques to make these calls to action work better. For attention to turn into action, it's important to make CTAs that get people to act right away. This chapter is essential for changing people's behavior.

Chapter 8: Data-Driven Creativity, the balance between using data and trusting your creative instincts, was talked about. We talked about how data can help and guide the creative process without stopping new ideas from coming up. Real-time data analytics and insights help make campaigns more effective and make sure that creative strategies are both well-thought-out and unique.

Chapter 9: Ethics and Authenticity in Modern Advertising talked about how important it is for businesses to be honest and take real responsibility for their actions. As people become less trusting, it's important to build trust and credibility through moral behavior and genuine support for social issues. This chapter talked about how ethical concerns and a real commitment to social issues can help your brand's image and help you connect with customers more deeply.

Chapter 10: Future-Proofing Your Advertising Strategies is excited about how new ideas and trends will shape the future of advertising. We looked into how environmental issues, AI, and augmented reality are changing the business. This chapter stressed how important it is to keep up with the latest news, be flexible, and use new technologies while keeping your brand's core character.

Basically, this book has given you all the information you need to get around in the complicated world of advertising. Understanding the consumer, making an emotional connection, embracing simplicity, building a strong brand identity, using stories, picking the right channels, writing compelling calls to action, balancing data with creativity, and being ethical are some of the most important rules that advertising should always follow. Marketers can make ads that not only get people's attention but also help them connect with them in a deep way by using these concepts along with a forward-thinking approach.

As advertising changes all the time, keeping ahead means being committed to always learning and adapting. Take advantage of the chances and challenges that come your way, and keep pushing the limits of what is possible in terms of creativity and efficiency. This book gives you the knowledge and tips you need to do well in this fast-paced field and make advertising efforts that stand out, connect with people deeply, and lead to success.

The End: of a Beginning

"*Success in advertising isn't about playing it safe or following the rules—it's about pushing limits, testing relentlessly, and turning every failure into a stepping stone for growth.*"

– Aman Verma

I hope you like the content of this book. If not, kindly give me feedback from whatever source you purchased it from. If you bought it from the store, you can email me at contact@theamanverma.com.

While much of this book has focused on merging creativity with data, the next phase is about throwing convention out the window and concentrating on what truly matters: hardcore selling and building a brand from scratch. This chapter is for the hustlers, the ones who aim not just to succeed but to dominate their niche.

It's time to get down to business—no fluff, no basics, only 100% executable, copy-paste concepts. I'm going to share personal case studies and strategies that I've used to scale from to₹1 crore in monthly revenue. This is about leaping from having nothing to running a brand that not only sustains itself but thrives in the competitive market. The principles that follow aren't just concepts; they're tried, tested, and optimized over years of real-world application. They go beyond theory, showing you exactly how I scaled campaigns by meticulously testing, scaling, and optimizing ads.

BREAKING THE MOLD: BUILD BRAND IN LESS THAN A YEAR

Many existing marketing theories assume that you need years to build a brand or that scaling requires massive budgets. I'm here to tell you that's a myth. Traditional models focus too much on the long game, but what about now? If you're starting with zero, there's no time for philosophical debates on brand identity or years of gradual growth. We're talking about hardcore selling, where you aim to hit your first ₹1 crore in sales as quickly as possible.

This requires an approach that combines ruthless testing with aggressive scaling. Forget about slow and steady. In today's digital

AI age, you can test, scale, and optimize in real time—adjusting your strategy day by day or even hour by hour.

WHAT'S NEXT?

This book was just the beginning. The next installment will dive even deeper into the mechanics of scaling brands from scratch—how to go from ₹0 to ₹1 crore and beyond. As we transition into a world where AI and automation rule, we'll break down the sophisticated strategies for large-scale growth, share more in-depth case studies, and discuss the future of advertising.

But remember: all of this starts with mastering the basics of hardcore selling, relentless testing, and aggressive scaling. Now go out there and make it happen.

www.ingramcontent.com/pod-product-compliance
Lightning Source LLC
LaVergne TN
LVHW021157160826
845679LV00024B/2145